T0252273

Cybersecurity in Intelligent Networking Systems

Cybersecurity in Intelligent Networking Systems

Shengjie Xu
San Diego State University, USA

Yi Qian
University of Nebraska-Lincoln, USA

Rose Qingyang Hu
Utah State University, USA

This edition first published 2023
© 2023 John Wiley & Sons Ltd

The right of Shengjie Xu, Yi Qian, and Rose Qingyang Hu to be identified as the authors of this work has been asserted in accordance with law.

Registered Offices
John Wiley & Sons, Inc., 111 River Street, Hoboken, NJ 07030, USA
John Wiley & Sons Ltd, The Atrium, Southern Gate, Chichester, West Sussex, PO19 8SQ, UK

For details of our global editorial offices, customer services, and more information about Wiley products visit us at www.wiley.com.

Wiley also publishes its books in a variety of electronic formats and by print-on-demand. Some content that appears in standard print versions of this book may not be available in other formats.

Library of Congress Cataloging-in-Publication Data
Names: Xu, Shengjie (Professor), author. | Qian, Yi, 1962- author. | Hu,
    Rose Qingyang, author.
Title: Cybersecurity in intelligent networking systems / Shengjie Xu, Yi
    Qian, Rose Qingyang Hu.
Description: Chichester, West Sussex, UK : Wiley, [2023] | Includes
    bibliographical references and index.
Identifiers: LCCN 2022033498 (print) | LCCN 2022033499 (ebook) | ISBN
    9781119783916 (hardback) | ISBN 9781119784104 (adobe pdf) | ISBN
    9781119784128 (epub)
Subjects: LCSH: Computer networks–Security measures.
Classification: LCC TK5105.59 .X87 2023 (print) | LCC TK5105.59 (ebook) |
    DDC 005.8–dc23/eng/20220826
LC record available at https://lccn.loc.gov/2022033498
LC ebook record available at https://lccn.loc.gov/2022033499

Cover Design: Wiley
Cover Image: © jijomathaidesigners/Shutterstock

Set in 9.5/12.5pt STIXTwoText by Straive, Chennai, India
Printed and bound by CPI Group (UK) Ltd, Croydon, CR0 4YY

C9781119783916_221022

Contents

About the Authors *xi*
Preface *xii*
Acknowledgments *xiv*
Acronyms *xv*

1   **Cybersecurity in the Era of Artificial Intelligence** *1*
1.1   Artificial Intelligence for Cybersecurity *2*
1.1.1   Artificial Intelligence *2*
1.1.2   Machine Learning *3*
1.1.2.1   Supervised Learning *3*
1.1.2.2   Unsupervised Learning *3*
1.1.2.3   Semi-supervised Learning *4*
1.1.2.4   Reinforcement Learning *4*
1.1.3   Data-Driven Workflow for Cybersecurity *4*
1.2   Key Areas and Challenges *5*
1.2.1   Anomaly Detection *5*
1.2.2   Trustworthy Artificial Intelligence *6*
1.2.3   Privacy Preservation *7*
1.3   Toolbox to Build Secure and Intelligent Systems *8*
1.3.1   Machine Learning and Deep Learning *8*
1.3.1.1   NumPy *8*
1.3.1.2   SciPy *8*
1.3.1.3   Scikit-learn *8*
1.3.1.4   PyTorch *8*
1.3.1.5   TensorFlow *9*
1.3.2   Privacy-Preserving Machine Learning *9*
1.3.2.1   Syft *9*
1.3.2.2   TensorFlow Federated *9*
1.3.2.3   TensorFlow Privacy *9*

1.3.3   Adversarial Machine Learning   *9*
1.3.3.1   SecML and SecML Malware   *9*
1.3.3.2   Foolbox   *10*
1.3.3.3   CleverHans   *10*
1.3.3.4   Counterfit   *10*
1.3.3.5   MintNV   *10*
1.4   Data Repositories for Cybersecurity Research   *10*
1.4.1   NSL-KDD   *10*
1.4.2   UNSW-NB15   *11*
1.4.3   EMBER   *11*
1.5   Summary   *11*
           Notes   *12*
           References   *12*

2   Cyber Threats and Gateway Defense   *17*
2.1   Cyber Threats   *17*
2.1.1   Cyber Intrusions   *17*
2.1.2   Distributed Denial of Services Attack   *19*
2.1.3   Malware and Shellcode   *19*
2.2   Gateway Defense Approaches   *20*
2.2.1   Network Access Control   *20*
2.2.2   Anomaly Isolation   *20*
2.2.3   Collaborative Learning   *20*
2.2.4   Secure Local Data Learning   *22*
2.3   Emerging Data-driven Methods for Gateway Defense   *22*
2.3.1   Semi-supervised Learning for Intrusion Detection   *22*
2.3.2   Transfer Learning for Intrusion Detection   *23*
2.3.3   Federated Learning for Privacy Preservation   *23*
2.3.4   Reinforcement Learning for Penetration Test   *24*
2.4   Case Study: Reinforcement Learning for Automated Post-breach
           Penetration Test   *24*
2.4.1   Literature Review   *25*
2.4.2   Research Idea   *25*
2.4.3   Training Agent Using Deep *Q*-Learning   *26*
2.5   Summary   *27*
           References   *27*

3   Edge Computing and Secure Edge Intelligence   *31*
3.1   Edge Computing   *31*
3.2   Key Advances in Edge Computing   *33*
3.2.1   Security   *33*

3.2.2   Reliability   *35*
3.2.3   Survivability   *36*
3.3   Secure Edge Intelligence   *36*
3.3.1   Background and Motivation   *37*
3.3.2   Design of Detection Module   *38*
3.3.2.1   Data Pre-processing   *38*
3.3.2.2   Model Learning   *38*
3.3.2.3   Model Updating   *39*
3.3.3   Challenges Against Poisoning Attacks   *40*
3.4   Summary   *40*
           References   *40*

4   Edge Intelligence for Intrusion Detection   *45*
4.1   Edge Cyberinfrastructure   *45*
4.2   Edge AI Engine   *46*
4.2.1   Feature Engineering   *47*
4.2.2   Model Learning   *48*
4.2.3   Model Update   *48*
4.2.4   Predictive Analytics   *49*
4.3   Threat Intelligence   *49*
4.4   Preliminary Study   *49*
4.4.1   Dataset   *49*
4.4.2   Environmental Setup   *50*
4.4.3   Performance Evaluation   *51*
4.4.3.1   Computational Efficiency   *51*
4.4.3.2   Prediction Accuracy   *52*
4.5   Summary   *53*
           References   *53*

5   Robust Intrusion Detection   *55*
5.1   Preliminaries   *55*
5.1.1   Median Absolute Deviation   *55*
5.1.2   Mahalanobis Distance   *55*
5.2   Robust Intrusion Detection   *56*
5.2.1   Problem Formulation   *56*
5.2.2   Step 1: Robust Data Pre-processing   *57*
5.2.3   Step 2: Bagging for Labeled Anomalies   *58*
5.2.4   Step 3: One-class SVM for Unlabeled Samples   *58*
5.2.4.1   One-class Classification   *59*
5.2.4.2   Algorithm of Optimal Sampling Ratio Section   *60*
5.2.5   Step 4: The Final Classifier   *61*

5.3   Experimental and Evaluation   *63*
5.3.1   Experiment Setup   *63*
5.3.1.1 Datasets   *63*
5.3.1.2 Environmental Setup   *64*
5.3.1.3 Evaluation Metrics   *64*
5.3.2   Performance Evaluation   *64*
5.3.2.1 Step 1   *64*
5.3.2.2 Step 2   *65*
5.3.2.3 Step 3   *65*
5.3.2.4 Step 4   *71*
5.4   Summary   *72*
         References   *72*

6   Efficient Pre-processing Scheme for Anomaly Detection   *75*
6.1   Efficient Anomaly Detection   *75*
6.1.1   Related Work   *76*
6.1.2   Principal Component Analysis   *77*
6.2   Proposed Pre-processing Scheme for Anomaly Detection   *78*
6.2.1   Robust Pre-processing Scheme   *79*
6.2.2   Real-Time Processing   *80*
6.2.3   Discussion   *82*
6.3   Case Study   *83*
6.3.1   Description of the Raw Data   *83*
6.3.1.1 Dimension   *83*
6.3.1.2 Predictors   *83*
6.3.1.3 Response Variables   *84*
6.3.2   Experiment   *84*
6.3.3   Results   *86*
6.4   Summary   *87*
         References   *87*

7   Privacy Preservation in the Era of Big Data   *91*
7.1   Privacy Preservation Approaches   *91*
7.1.1   Anonymization   *91*
7.1.2   Differential Privacy   *92*
7.1.3   Federated Learning   *93*
7.1.4   Homomorphic Encryption   *94*
7.1.5   Secure Multi-party Computation   *95*
7.1.6   Discussion   *96*

7.2 Privacy-Preserving Anomaly Detection *96*
7.2.1 Literature Review *97*
7.2.2 Preliminaries *99*
7.2.2.1 Bilinear Groups *99*
7.2.2.2 Asymmetric Predicate Encryption *99*
7.2.3 System Model and Security Model *99*
7.2.3.1 System Model *100*
7.2.3.2 Security Model *100*
7.3 Objectives and Workflow *101*
7.3.1 Objectives *101*
7.3.2 Workflow *102*
7.4 Predicate Encryption-Based Anomaly Detection *103*
7.4.1 Procedures *103*
7.4.2 Development of Predicate *104*
7.4.3 Deployment of Anomaly Detection *105*
7.5 Case Study and Evaluation *106*
7.5.1 Overhead *106*
7.5.2 Detection *106*
7.6 Summary *109*
  References *109*

8 **Adversarial Examples: Challenges and Solutions** *113*
8.1 Adversarial Examples *113*
8.1.1 Problem Formulation in Machine Learning *113*
8.1.2 Creation of Adversarial Examples *114*
8.1.3 Targeted and Non-targeted Attacks *114*
8.1.4 Black-box and White-box Attacks *115*
8.1.5 Defenses Against Adversarial Examples *115*
8.2 Adversarial Attacks in Security Applications *115*
8.2.1 Malware *115*
8.2.2 Cyber Intrusions *116*
8.3 Case Study: Improving Adversarial Attacks Against Malware Detectors *116*
8.3.1 Background *116*
8.3.2 Adversarial Attacks on Malware Detectors *117*
8.3.3 MalConv Architecture *118*
8.3.4 Research Idea *119*
8.4 Case Study: A Metric for Machine Learning Vulnerability to Adversarial Examples *119*
8.4.1 Background *120*

8.4.2   Research Idea   *120*
8.5   Case Study: Protecting Smart Speakers from Adversarial Voice
          Commands   *122*
8.5.1   Background   *122*
8.5.2   Challenges   *122*
8.5.3   Directions and Tasks   *123*
8.6   Summary   *124*
          References   *124*

          Index   *127*

About the Authors

Shengjie Xu, PhD, is an assistant professor in the Management Information Systems Department at San Diego State University, USA. He is a recipient of the IET Journals Premium Award for Best Paper in 2020, the Milton E. Mohr Graduate Fellowship Award from the University of Nebraska–Lincoln in 2017, and the Best Poster Award from the International Conference on Design of Reliable Communication Networks in 2015. He serves as a Technical Editor for *IEEE Wireless Communications* Magazine. He holds multiple professional certifications in cybersecurity and computer networking.

Yi Qian, PhD, is a professor in the Department of Electrical and Computer Engineering at the University of Nebraska–Lincoln, USA. He is a recipient of the Henry Y. Kleinkauf Family Distinguished New Faculty Teaching Award in 2011, the Holling Family Distinguished Teaching Award in 2012, the Holling Family Distinguished Teaching/Advising/Mentoring Award in 2018, and the Holling Family Distinguished Teaching Award for Innovative Use of Instructional Technology in 2018, all from the University of Nebraska–Lincoln, USA.

Rose Qingyang Hu, PhD, is a professor in the Department of Electrical and Computer Engineering and Associate Dean of Research in the College of Engineering at Utah State University, USA. She is a recipient of outstanding faculty researcher of the year in 2014 and 2016 and outstanding graduate mentor of the year in 2022, all from Utah State University, USA. She is a Fellow of IEEE, IEEE ComSoc Distinguished Lecturer 2015–2018, IEEE VTS Distinguished Lecturer 2020–2022.

Preface

Nowadays, malicious attacks and emerging cyber threats have been inducing catastrophic damage to critical infrastructure and causing widespread outages. There are three major types of cyberattacks that are compromising modern networking systems: (i) *Attacks targeting Confidentiality* intend to acquire unauthorized information from network resources; (ii) *Attacks targeting Integrity* aim at deliberately and illegally modifying or disrupting data exchange; and (iii) *Attacks targeting Availability* attempt to delay, block or corrupt service delivery. Confidentiality, integrity, and availability are the three pillars of cybersecurity. It is urgent to defend critical networking systems against any forms of cyber threats from adversaries.

The rapid and successful advances of intelligent discoveries offer security researchers and practitioners new platforms to investigate challenging issues emerging in several networking systems. Those intelligent solutions will boost the efficiency and effectiveness of multiple critical security applications. Motivated by the current technological advances, this book intends to offer the current research challenges in the field of cybersecurity, as well as some novel security solutions that make critical networking systems secure, robust, and intelligent. Specifically, the book focuses on cybersecurity and its intersections with artificial intelligence, machine learning, edge computing, and privacy preservation. There are eight chapters in the book.

Chapter 1 deals with cybersecurity in the era of artificial intelligence and machine learning. The chapter first introduces the concepts of artificial intelligence and machine learning. It then illustrates some key advances and challenges in cybersecurity, including anomaly detection, trustworthy artificial intelligence, and privacy preservation. Toolbox to build secure and intelligent systems is then presented. The chapter then demonstrates a few data repositories for cybersecurity research.

Chapter 2 deals with cyber threats and defense mechanisms. The chapter first illustrates multiple effective gateway defense methods against cyber threats. It then presents a research study that innovates reinforcement learning for penetration test.

Chapter 3 deals with edge computing. Edge computing is presented to highlight its key advances and unique capabilities in communication networks. The chapter then illustrates the concept of secure edge intelligence.

Chapter 4 deals with edge intelligence for intrusion detection. The systematic design of edge intelligence is first presented. Three main modules in edge intelligence are illustrated. The chapter then demonstrates a case study including experiment and evaluation.

Chapter 5 deals with a robust intrusion detection scheme. The preliminaries of robust statistics are first introduced. The chapter then presents the details of the proposed scheme. An experimental study and evaluation are then demonstrated.

Chapter 6 deals with an efficient processing scheme for anomaly detection. A few related studies and background of principal component analysis are first introduced. It then presents the proposed efficient preprocessing scheme for anomaly detection, whose objective is to achieve high detection accuracy while learning from the preprocessed data. The chapter then demonstrates a case study including experiment and evaluation.

Chapter 7 deals with privacy preservation in the era of big data. A few modern privacy-preserving approaches are first illustrated. It then presents a proposed scheme that focuses on detecting anomalous behaviors in a privacy-preserving way. The chapter offers an experimental study and evaluation.

Chapter 8 deals with adversarial examples and adversarial machine learning. The concept of adversarial examples and its challenges are first introduced. Three research studies in adversarial examples are then presented from both offensive and defensive perspectives.

We hope that our readers will enjoy this book.

Shengjie Xu, San Diego State University
Yi Qian, University of Nebraska–Lincoln
Rose Qingyang Hu, Utah State University

Acknowledgments

First, we would like to thank our families for their love and support.

We would like to thank our colleagues and students at Dakota State University, University of Nebraska-Lincoln, Utah State University, and San Diego State University for their support and enthusiasm in this book project and this topic.

We express our thanks to the staff at Wiley for their support. We would like to thank Sandra Grayson, Juliet Booker, and Becky Cowan for their patience in handling publication issues.

This book project was partially supported by the U.S. National Science Foundation under grants CNS-1423348, CNS-1423408, EARS-1547312, and EARS-1547330.

Acronyms

ABE	attributed based encryption
AE	adversarial examples
AES	Advanced Encryption Standard
AI	artificial intelligence
AML	adversarial machine learning
API	application programming interface
APT	advanced persistent threats
ASR	automatic speech recognition
CDN	content delivery network
CPS	cyber physical system
CPU	central processing unit
CSV	comma-separated values
DBSCAN	density-based spatial clustering of applications with noise
DDOS	distributed denial of service
DL	deep learning
DNN	deep neural network
DOS	denial of service
DP	differential privacy
FGSM	fast gradient sign method
FL	federated learning
GAN	generative adversarial networks
GDPR	General Data Protection Regulation
GPU	graphics processing unit
HE	homomorphic encryption
ICT	information and communication technology
IDS	intrusion detection system
IOT	Internet of Things
IP	Internet Protocol

IQR	interquartile range
JSON	JavaScript object notation
LAN	local area network
LDA	linear discriminant analysis
MAD	median absolute deviation
MD	Mahalanobis distance
MER	mean error rate
ML	machine learning
NIDS	network intrusion detection system
NIST	National Institute of Standards and Technology
ODE	ordinary differential equations
PC	principal component
PCA	principal component analysis
PE	portable executable
POMDP	partially observable Markov decision process
PVE	proportion of variance explained
QOE	quality of experience
RAM	random access memory
SMPC	secure multi-party computation
TA	trusted authority
TCP	transmission control protocol
TPU	tensor processing unit

1

Cybersecurity in the Era of Artificial Intelligence

The rapid and successful advances of artificial intelligence (AI) and machine learning (ML) offer security researchers and practitioners new approaches and platforms to explore and investigate challenging issues emerging in many safety-critical systems. Those AI/ML-enabled solutions have boosted the efficiency and effectiveness of multiple important security applications. For example, recent advances in AI and ML have been widely applied in intrusion detection system (IDS) (Xu et al., 2017, 2019a,b, 2020), malware detection system (Bradley and Xu, 2021; Bradley, 2022; Ahmed and Xu, 2022), and penetration testing (Chaudhary et al., 2020).

However, the rise of AI and ML is often considered as a "double-edged sword." While AI and ML can be adopted to identify threats more accurately and prevent cyberattacks more efficiently, cybersecurity professionals must respond to the increasingly sophisticated motivations from adversaries. Modern intelligent networking systems have been maliciously manipulated, evaded, and misled, causing significant security incidents in financial systems, cyber-physical systems, and many other critical domains. Threat actors and adversarial attackers have been applying techniques to carry out adversarial attacks targeting various AI/ML-enabled networking systems (Burr and Xu, 2021; Burr, 2022). For instance, an adversary can inject well-designed audio signals to confuse the voice recognition systems in smart speakers to deliver random noises, or compromising the self-driving vehicles by creating visual alterations of the stop sign, leaving the ML model erroneously identify a stop sign as a speed limit sign with 70 miles per hour (mph) (Yuan et al., 2019). Those adversarial attacks could lead to unauthorized disclosure of sensitive information, affect the safety and wellness of users, and thwart Internet freedom. Therefore, cybersecurity professionals must evolve rapidly as technology advances and new cyber threats emerge.

Cybersecurity in Intelligent Networking Systems, First Edition.
Shengjie Xu, Yi Qian, and Rose Qingyang Hu.
© 2023 John Wiley & Sons Ltd. Published 2023 by John Wiley & Sons Ltd.

1.1 Artificial Intelligence for Cybersecurity

The concepts of AI and ML are firstly introduced, followed by the data-driven workflow for cybersecurity tasks.

1.1.1 Artificial Intelligence

The phrase *AI* is popularly discussed worldwide. Nowadays, AI generally refers to the simulation of human intelligent behavior by computational models to make decisions, and it is a rapidly evolving field of study, research, and application that is being used to improve economic development, modern human lifestyle, and national security. Along with recent technological advances, AI is used for innovation in various critical domains, such as robotics, manufacturing, business, finance, and many others.

AI applications are primarily enabled by *ML*, which is considered as the pillar of AI's success. Many organizations treat ML as the main approach to implement AI applications. It is an exciting field involving multiple subjects, including statistics, computer science, business management, linguistics, and more. Traditionally speaking, ML refers to the process of learning and understanding from historical data, mining and extracting the valuable information by recognizing the pattern and relationship, making decisions, and forecasting outcomes, trends, and behaviors. It involves a vast set of statistical models and tools, including generalized linear models, tree-based methods, neural networks, support vector machines, and nearest neighbors. Nowadays, ML is boosted by Big Data, massive computing power, and advanced learning models. In a technical article (Copeland, 2018), the author uses a Venn diagram to describe AI, ML, deep learning (DL), and their relationship. In Figure 1.1, the broad concept of AI including ML and DL is displayed. Currently, DL is leading the field of AI and ML, and it has made a significant number of progresses in a variety of ML domains, such as image classification, speech recognition, and object recognition.

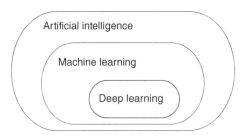

Figure 1.1 Artificial intelligence, machine learning, and deep learning.

Table 1.1 Example of a house price dataset.

(x_0)	(x_1)	(x_2)	(x_3)	...	(y)
Index	Number of bedrooms	Square footage (sqft)	Number of bathrooms	...	Price ($)
1	2	1600	2	...	≈ 250 000
2	4	2200	5	...	≈ 550 000
3	3	1800	3	...	≈ 400 000
...	...	...	...	...	...
100	4	2100	4	...	≈ 450 000

1.1.2 Machine Learning

ML offers computers to learn by mining massive datasets. Here, four broad categories of ML are described. They are supervised learning, unsupervised learning, semi-supervised learning, and reinforcement learning.

1.1.2.1 Supervised Learning

Most of the ML problems fall into supervised or unsupervised. For instance, there is a house pricing dataset (Table 1.1), in which each row (observation) represents a house and each column (feature) represents an attribute (e.g. number of bedrooms). For each observation, an associated target value is shown. Here, the objective is to build a model that captures the relationship between the target value y (price) and the attributes $(x_0, \dots, x_3)$ so that accurate predictions for future observations can be achieved.

Supervised learning addresses this type of problem by training the model with features and labeled data (y). A supervised learning model takes a set of known input data (features) and known output data (response/target) and trains a model to make reasonable predictions for the response to new data. Regression and classification are the main categories for supervised learning problems. In regression problems, there are many classical models available for training, including linear regression, ordinal regression, and neural network regression. In classification problems, there are also many classical models available for training, including logistic regression, tree-based methods, support vector machine, random forest, and boosting methods.

1.1.2.2 Unsupervised Learning

Unsupervised learning trains the model with unlabeled data. Its goal is to unveil the patterns in the data. Unsupervised learning serves as a good approach to simplify the data by reducing the dimensionality, finding similar groups, and perceiving intrinsic structures. Clustering and dimensionality reduction are the main categories for unsupervised learning problems. In clustering problems, there are many classical models available for training, including K-means, Density-Based Spatial Clustering of Applications with Noise (DBSCAN), and hierarchical clustering. In dimensionality reduction problems, there are also many classical models available for training, including principal component analysis (PCA) and linear discriminant analysis (LDA).

1.1.2.3 Semi-supervised Learning

Semi-supervised learning deals with partially labeled data, which typically consist of a small amount of labeled and a large amount of unlabeled data. It falls between supervised learning, where completely labeled data are needed, and unsupervised learning, where no labeled data are needed. The trained model from semi-supervised learning can be highly accurate. Semi-supervised learning is also widely applied in the field of cybersecurity, especially in anomaly detection.

1.1.2.4 Reinforcement Learning

Reinforcement learning is a unique ML paradigm. This model learns a series of actions by maximizing a Reward Function f. The function f can be maximized by penalizing "bad action" and/or rewarding "good action." In the reinforcement learning setting, an agent takes actions in an environment that is treated as a reward and a representation of the state that is fed back to the agent. There are many popular examples that are enabled by reinforcement learning, such as self-driving vehicles (Gyawali et al., 2020) and AlphaGo (Silver et al., 2017).

1.1.3 Data-Driven Workflow for Cybersecurity

In the field of cybersecurity, data-driven methods are playing a crucial role in cybersecurity tasks, such as threat intelligence, risk analysis, vulnerability testing, and defense against adversarial behaviors. Figure 1.2 presents the general data-driven workflow to solve cybersecurity problems. The first step starts from formulating a concrete security problem and justifying the need to apply data-driven methods. For example, security practitioners can start defining a problem about intrusion detection, analyze the possible outputs given the inputs, and then argue whether data-driven methods are appropriate to automate the task. In the second step, data collection and preprocessing are conducted. Data acquisition is essential, and it is important to assure

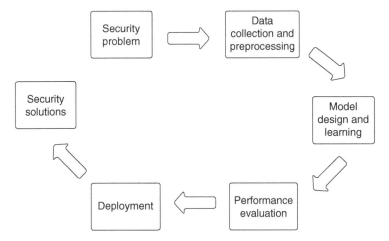

Figure 1.2 Data-driven workflow for cybersecurity.

that not only sufficient data are collected but also labeling and data sampling are correct and unbiased. In the third step, ML and other statistical models are designed and trained. It is important to assure that the trained model can be generalized well to future data and even unseen data. In the fourth step, performance evaluation is conducted to assess the quality of the trained model. Model assessment should be carried out by using suitable baseline data and appropriate metrics. In the fifth step, model deployment is performed. It is crucial to note that the deployment should perform well outside of a lab environment, and it should also work well under different settings in various threat models. Lastly, a mature and robust security solution for learning-based IDS is released.

1.2 Key Areas and Challenges

The research communities have been actively exploring both the offense and defense sides of data-driven cybersecurity. As more achievements are accomplished, several research challenges that emerge rapidly are pending to be solved. Here, three aspects are described. They are anomaly detection, trustworthy AI, and privacy preservation.

1.2.1 Anomaly Detection

In the context of cybersecurity, anomalies refer to those abnormal behaviors that harm the information systems. To defend against them, anomaly detection focuses on identifying anomalous behaviors during a period of operations. This can be extended to a few use cases in security, such as intrusion detection, malware detection, phishing detection, spam detection, and defense against zero-day attack.

The goal of intrusion detection is to examine traffic data and classify normal activities and attack behaviors (Xu et al., 2019). More topics about cyber intrusions and intrusion detection will be covered in detail in Chapters 2, 4, 5, and 6.

Malware has been near the forefront of modern cybersecurity issues (Ahmed and Xu, 2022). The detection and prevention of malware has become a major challenge. In many cases, antivirus tools such as Windows Defender utilize ML to scan files and detect malicious patterns. With the recent trend of ransomware cases around the world, it has become more important than ever to have effective anti-malware to keep users and organizations safe. Modern malware can take many forms. It can be embedded in document macros, run as shellcode, and much more. Malware is also versatile in the taskings it can complete. It can implant a command-and-control server (C2) beacon, install a keylogger, or ransom a computer by encrypting all of the files. In addition to completing malicious tasks, malware has a secondary objective of avoiding detection by disguising itself as a valid process on a computer and obfuscate the detector.

Phishing is a tactic that is used by threat actors to achieve their goals, such as obtaining credentials of employees or delivering malware (Khonji et al., 2013). With the prevalence of these types of attacks, it is important to detect and stop the attacks at any point in their lifecycle. Being able to detect that a website is likely a phishing site could be a useful tool in mitigating the success of the attacks.

In recent years, the poisoning attack has become a new form of attack to compromise networking systems and the learning models they integrate. Data poisoning attack is the intentional act of polluting data that the algorithms need to train (Huang et al., 2021). It can impact organizations as well as individuals in a negative manner. Some real-life examples of this type of attack include an attacker changing what an email spam filter might mark as spam. This would allow an attacker to send any kind of email they want without being flagged. Similarly, there are firewall tools that use ML to monitor network traffic and look for malware entering the network. An attacker could use a similar method to evade detection.

1.2.2 Trustworthy Artificial Intelligence

Most of the AI/ML models face the issue of being trustworthy because they are vulnerable to various kinds of attacks (e.g. adversarial examples)

(Li et al., 2021a,b). This is because they are not yet explainable owing to the black-box nature of many AI/ML models, especially DL models (Zou et al., 2021), and their uncertainty has not been quantified (Li et al., 2021c). This highlights the importance of additional research activities in the trustworthiness of AI/ML models. Moreover, more studies are needed to systematically understand the trustworthiness of AI/ML models, as well as to advance the state-of-the-art trustworthiness, robustness, and interpretability of AI/ML.

Currently, research challenges of trustworthy AI and adversarial ML include, but not limited to, the following aspects: quantifying trustworthiness of AI/ML methods against sophisticated attacks, such as adversarial examples, poisoning attacks, or evasive attacks; determining the conditions to whether trust AI/ML models or not; explaining and interpreting recommendations made by AI/ML models; detecting and mitigating adversarial examples against AI/ML models; and enhancing trustworthiness of AI/ML models by incorporating countermeasures. Trustworthy AI and adversarial ML will be covered in detail in Chapter 8.

1.2.3 Privacy Preservation

The protection of sensitive data is critical. In the field of health study, the data privacy problem is growing because of the challenges in data privacy regulations, privacy leakage by attackers, and the pervasive data mining operations. In one study (Na et al., 2018), the authors discussed that by utilizing large national physical activity datasets, the children and adults were reidentified by ML when 20 minute data with several pieces of demographic information were used. Unfortunately, more incidents are reported worldwide regarding privacy leakage. With the enforcement of General Data Protection Regulation (GDPR) (Voigt and Von dem Bussche, 2017), companies and organizations will need to comply with specific terms and conditions to protect the data privacy of European Union citizens.

The increasing attention on security and privacy has motivated the rapid design and implementation of multiple privacy-preserving methods. For instance, federated learning (FL) was designed to train ML models across multiple end nodes without sharing the local data to a centralized server. One article shared that Google has implemented a mobile application that offers privacy-preserving word prediction-based FL (Hard et al., 2018).

There are a few modern approaches for privacy preservation, including anonymization, differential privacy (DP), homomorphic encryption (HE), and secure multi-party computation (SMPC). These approaches will be covered in detail in Chapter 7.

1.3 Toolbox to Build Secure and Intelligent Systems

A few scientific computing tools are commonly utilized as the toolbox to build intelligent systems. Here, a few Python libraries are described. They are for ML and DL, privacy-preserving ML, and adversarial ML.

1.3.1 Machine Learning and Deep Learning

Five Python libraries are widely used for ML and scientific computing. They are NumPy,[1] SciPy,[2] scikit-learn,[3] PyTorch,[4] and TensorFlow.[5]

1.3.1.1 NumPy

NumPy is the fundamental library for scientific computing in Python. It is a Python library that provides a multi-dimensional array object, various derived objects (such as masked arrays and matrices), and an assortment of routines for fast operations on arrays, including mathematical, logical, shape manipulation, sorting, selecting, I/O, discrete Fourier transforms, basic linear algebra, basic statistical operations, random simulation, and much more (Harris et al., 2020).

1.3.1.2 SciPy

SciPy is a Python library for mathematics, science, and engineering. It includes modules for statistics, optimization, integration, linear algebra, Fourier transforms, signal and image processing, ordinary differential equations (ODE) solvers, and more (Virtanen et al., 2020). SciPy is built to work with NumPy arrays and provides many user-friendly and efficient numerical routines, such as routines for numerical integration and optimization.

1.3.1.3 Scikit-learn

Scikit-learn is a Python library for ML built on top of SciPy (Pedregosa et al., 2011). It offers multiple modules for ML tasks, including classification, regression, clustering, dimensionality reduction, model selection, and preprocessing.

1.3.1.4 PyTorch

PyTorch is an optimized tensor library for DL. It provides deep neural networks built on an automatic differentiation system (autograd), as well as tensor computation with strong graphics processing unit (GPU) acceleration.

It can be used either as a replacement for NumPy to use the power of GPUs or a DL research platform that provides maximum flexibility and speed (Paszke et al., 2019).

1.3.1.5 TensorFlow

TensorFlow is an open-source platform for ML and DL. It has a comprehensive, flexible ecosystem of tools, libraries, and community resources that lets researchers push the state-of-the-art in ML and developers easily build and deploy ML-powered applications (Abadi et al., 2016).

1.3.2 Privacy-Preserving Machine Learning

Three Python libraries are widely used for privacy-preserving ML. They are Syft,[6] TensorFlow Federated,[7] and TensorFlow Privacy.[8]

1.3.2.1 Syft

Syft is a Python library that preserves the privacy of data from model training, using FL, DP, and SMPC and HE within the main DL frameworks such as PyTorch and TensorFlow (Ziller et al., 2021).

1.3.2.2 TensorFlow Federated

TensorFlow Federated is an open-source framework for ML and other computations on decentralized data. It has been developed to facilitate open research and experimentation with FL (TFF, 2018).

1.3.2.3 TensorFlow Privacy

TensorFlow Privacy is a Python library that includes implementations of TensorFlow optimizers for training ML models with DP (TFP, 2022). The library contains a set of tutorials on building a language model with DP, learning a DL model with DP, and learning a differentially private logistic regression model on data.

1.3.3 Adversarial Machine Learning

Six Python libraries are widely used for adversarial ML. They are SecML,[9] SecML Malware,[10] Foolbox,[11] CleverHans,[12] Counterfit,[13] and MintNV.[14]

1.3.3.1 SecML and SecML Malware

SecML is a Python library for the security evaluation of ML models. It contains a set of ML models, built-in attack algorithms, pre-trained models, multi-processing, and more. It offers tutorials in evasion attack, poisoning attack, and interpretability examples in ML (Melis et al., 2019). SecML Malware is a Python library for creating adversarial attacks against Windows Malware detectors. Built on top of SecML, it includes most attacks proposed in key articles (Demetrio and Biggio, 2021).

1.3.3.2 Foolbox

Foolbox is a Python library to create adversarial examples that fool ML models such as neural networks, as well as quantify and compare the robustness of ML models (Rauber et al., 2020). It is built because the most comparable robustness measure is the minimum perturbation needed to craft an adversarial example (Rauber et al., 2017).

1.3.3.3 CleverHans

CleverHans is a Python library to benchmark the vulnerability of ML systems to adversarial examples (Papernot et al., 2016).

1.3.3.4 Counterfit

Counterfit is a command-line tool and generic automation layer for assessing the security of ML systems (Counterfit, 2022).

1.3.3.5 MintNV

MintNV AI/ML educational exercise is a vulnerable environment for security professionals to practice attacking ML applications. This environment will locally host a realistic website and server for the end user to compromise (MintNV, 2022). Counterfit can be enabled within MintNV.

1.4   Data Repositories for Cybersecurity Research

Data are crucial for cybersecurity in the era of AI. A researcher created a site[15] that offers sources to multiple security-related data. Here, three datasets for cybersecurity research are described.

1.4.1   NSL-KDD

The NSL-KDD data are for intrusion detection problem (Revathi and Malathi, 2013). It was updated from data at the Third International Knowledge Discovery and Data Mining Tools Competition (KDD Cup 1999 data), which was to build a network intrusion detector, a predictive model capable of distinguishing between "bad" connections, called intrusions or attacks, and "good" normal connections. The KDD data were created in an environment to acquire nine weeks of raw TCP dump data for a local area network (LAN) simulating a typical U.S. Air Force LAN (Stolfo et al., 2000). A connection is a sequence of TCP packets in which the data flow to and from a source IP address to a target IP address under some well-defined protocol. Each connection is labeled as either normal or as an attack with exactly one specific attack type. Attacks fall into four main categories: DoS: denial-of-service, e.g. syn flood; R2L: unauthorized access from a remote machine, e.g. guessing password; U2R: unauthorized access to local superuser (root) privileges, e.g. various "buffer overflow" attacks; and probing: surveillance and other probing, e.g. port scanning (Stolfo et al., 2000).

1.4.2 UNSW-NB15

The raw network packets of the UNSW-NB15 dataset were created in the Cyber Range Lab of University of New South Wales (UNSW) Canberra for generating a hybrid of real modern normal activities and synthetic contemporary attack behaviors (Moustafa and Slay, 2015). The tcpdump tool was utilized to capture 100 GB of the raw traffic (e.g. pcap files). This dataset has nine types of attacks, including Fuzzers, Analysis, Backdoors, DoS, Exploits, Generic, Reconnaissance, Shellcode, and Worms (Moustafa and Slay, 2016).

1.4.3 EMBER

EMBER dataset (Elastic Malware Benchmark for Empowering Researchers) is a collection of features from PE files that serve as a benchmark dataset. It focuses specifically on PE files, containing features and labels from 1.1 million samples. The data are packaged in JavaScript Object Notation (JSON). The labels are spread evenly as well, with an equal number of malicious and benign samples. Unlabeled samples are also included in the dataset. Raw features are extracted to JSON format and included in the publicly available dataset. Vectorized features can be produced from these raw features and saved in binary format from which they can be converted to CSV, dataframe, or any other format (Anderson and Roth, 2018).

1.5 Summary

In this chapter, the broader impact of AI and ML for cybersecurity is presented. The recent key research areas and challenges are discussed, and these areas will be illustrated in the following chapters. The toolbox for building secure and robust intelligent networking systems is introduced, and it can be designed, developed, and implemented by utilizing several datasets for cybersecurity research.

Notes

1 NumPy. https://numpy.org/
2 SciPy. https://scipy.org/
3 scikit-learn. https://scikit-learn.org/stable/
4 PyTorch. https://pytorch.org/
5 TensorFlow. https://www.tensorflow.org/
6 Syft. https://github.com/OpenMined/PySyft
7 TensorFlow Federated. https://www.tensorflow.org/federated
8 TensorFlow Privacy. https://github.com/tensorflow/privacy
9 SecML. https://secml.readthedocs.io/en/stable/index.html
10 SecML Malware. https://github.com/pralab/secml_malware
11 Foolbox. https://github.com/bethgelab/foolbox
12 CleverHans. https://github.com/cleverhans-lab/cleverhans
13 Counterfit. https://github.com/Azure/counterfit
14 MintNV. https://catalog.ngc.nvidia.com/orgs/nvidia/teams/product-security/containers/mintnv
15 Samples of Security-Related Data. https://www.secrepo.com

References

Martín Abadi, Paul Barham, Jianmin Chen, Zhifeng Chen, Andy Davis, Jeffrey Dean, Matthieu Devin, Sanjay Ghemawat, Geoffrey Irving, Michael Isard, et al. {TensorFlow}: A system for {Large-Scale} machine learning. In *12th USENIX Symposium on Operating Systems Design and Implementation (OSDI 16)*, pages 265–283, 2016.

Tarek Ahmed and Shengjie Xu. Shellcoding: Hunting for Kernel32 base address. In *IEEE INFOCOM 2022-IEEE Conference on Computer Communications Workshops (INFOCOM WKSHPS)*, pages 1–2. IEEE, 2022.

Hyrum S Anderson and Phil Roth. EMBER: An open dataset for training static PE malware machine learning models. *arXiv preprint arXiv:1804.04637*, 2018.

Matt Bradley. A metric for machine learning vulnerability to adversarial examples. *Dakota State University - Masters Theses & Doctoral Dissertations*, 2022.

Matthew Bradley and Shengjie Xu. A metric for machine learning vulnerability to adversarial examples. In *IEEE INFOCOM 2021-IEEE Conference on Computer Communications Workshops (INFOCOM WKSHPS)*, pages 1–2. IEEE, 2021.

Justin Burr. Improving adversarial attacks against MalConv. *Dakota State University - Masters Theses & Doctoral Dissertations*, 2022.

Justin Burr and Shengjie Xu. Improving adversarial attacks against executable raw byte classifiers. In *IEEE INFOCOM 2021-IEEE Conference on Computer Communications Workshops (INFOCOM WKSHPS)*, pages 1–2. IEEE, 2021.

Sujita Chaudhary, Austin O'Brien, and Shengjie Xu. Automated post-breach penetration testing through reinforcement learning. In *2020 IEEE Conference on Communications and Network Security (CNS)*, pages 1–2. IEEE, 2020.

Michael Copeland. What's the difference between artificial intelligence, machine learning and deep learning? 2018. URL https://blogs.nvidia.com/blog/2016/07/29/whats-difference-artificial-intelligence-machine-learning-deep-learning-ai/.

Counterfit. Counterfit, 2022. URL https://github.com/Azure/counterfit.

Luca Demetrio and Battista Biggio. Secml-malware: Pentesting windows malware classifiers with adversarial EXEmples in Python. *arXiv preprint arXiv:2104.12848*, 2021.

Sohan Gyawali, Shengjie Xu, Yi Qian, and Rose Qingyang Hu. Challenges and solutions for cellular based V2X communications. *IEEE Communication Surveys and Tutorials*, 23(1):222–255, 2020.

Andrew Hard, Kanishka Rao, Rajiv Mathews, Swaroop Ramaswamy, Françoise Beaufays, Sean Augenstein, Hubert Eichner, Chloé Kiddon, and Daniel Ramage. Federated learning for mobile keyboard prediction. *arXiv preprint arXiv:1811.03604*, 2018.

Charles R Harris, K Jarrod Millman, Stéfan J Van Der Walt, Ralf Gommers, Pauli Virtanen, David Cournapeau, Eric Wieser, Julian Taylor, Sebastian Berg, Nathaniel J Smith, et al. Array programming with NumPy. *Nature*, 585(7825):357–362, 2020.

Hai Huang, Jiaming Mu, Neil Zhenqiang Gong, Qi Li, Bin Liu, and Mingwei Xu. Data poisoning attacks to deep learning based recommender systems. *arXiv preprint arXiv:2101.02644*, 2021.

Mahmoud Khonji, Youssef Iraqi, and Andrew Jones. Phishing detection: A literature survey. *IEEE Communication Surveys and Tutorials*, 15(4):2091–2121, 2013.

Deqiang Li, Qianmu Li, Yanfang Ye, and Shouhuai Xu. Arms race in adversarial malware detection: A survey. *ACM Computing Surveys (CSUR)*, 55(1):1–35, 2021a.

Deqiang Li, Qianmu Li, Yanfang Ye, and Shouhuai Xu. A framework for enhancing deep neural networks against adversarial malware. *IEEE Transactions on Network Science and Engineering*, 8(1):736–750, 2021b.

Deqiang Li, Tian Qiu, Shuo Chen, Qianmu Li, and Shouhuai Xu. Can we leverage predictive uncertainty to detect dataset shift and adversarial examples in android malware detection? In *Annual Computer Security Applications Conference*, pages 596–608, 2021c.

Marco Melis, Ambra Demontis, Maura Pintor, Angelo Sotgiu, and Battista Biggio. secml: A python library for secure and explainable machine learning. *arXiv preprint arXiv:1912.10013*, 2019.

MintNV. MintNV, 6 2022. URL https://catalog.ngc.nvidia.com/orgs/nvidia/teams/product-security/containers/mintnv.

Nour Moustafa and Jill Slay. UNSW-NB15: A comprehensive data set for network intrusion detection systems (UNSW-NB15 network data set). In *Military Communications and Information Systems Conference (MilCIS), 2015*, pages 1–6. IEEE, 2015.

Nour Moustafa and Jill Slay. The evaluation of network anomaly detection systems: Statistical analysis of the UNSW-NB15 data set and the comparison with the KDD99 data set. *Information Security Journal: A Global Perspective*, 25(1–3):18–31, 2016.

Liangyuan Na, Cong Yang, Chi-Cheng Lo, Fangyuan Zhao, Yoshimi Fukuoka, and Anil Aswani. Feasibility of reidentifying individuals in large national physical activity data sets from which protected health information has been removed with use of machine learning. *JAMA Network Open*, 1(8):e186040, 2018.

Nicolas Papernot, Fartash Faghri, Nicholas Carlini, Ian Goodfellow, Reuben Feinman, Alexey Kurakin, Cihang Xie, Yash Sharma, Tom Brown, Aurko Roy, et al. Technical report on the cleverhans v2.1.0 adversarial examples library. *arXiv preprint arXiv:1610.00768*, 2016.

Adam Paszke, Sam Gross, Francisco Massa, Adam Lerer, James Bradbury, Gregory Chanan, Trevor Killeen, Zeming Lin, Natalia Gimelshein, Luca Antiga, et al. PyTorch: An imperative style, high-performance deep learning library. *Advances in Neural Information Processing Systems 32*, 2019.

Fabian Pedregosa, Gaël Varoquaux, Alexandre Gramfort, Vincent Michel, Bertrand Thirion, Olivier Grisel, Mathieu Blondel, Peter Prettenhofer, Ron Weiss, Vincent Dubourg, et al. Scikit-learn: Machine learning in python. *Journal of Machine Learning Research*, 12:2825–2830, 2011.

Jonas Rauber, Wieland Brendel, and Matthias Bethge. Foolbox: A python toolbox to benchmark the robustness of machine learning models. *arXiv preprint arXiv:1707.04131*, 2017.

Jonas Rauber, Roland Zimmermann, Matthias Bethge, and Wieland Brendel. Foolbox native: Fast adversarial attacks to benchmark the robustness of machine learning models in pytorch, tensorflow, and jax. *Journal of Open Source Software*, 5(53):2607, 2020.

S Revathi and A Malathi. A detailed analysis on NSL-KDD dataset using various machine learning techniques for intrusion detection. *International Journal of Engineering Research & Technology (IJERT)*, 2(12):1848–1853, 2013.

David Silver, Julian Schrittwieser, Karen Simonyan, Ioannis Antonoglou, Aja Huang, Arthur Guez, Thomas Hubert, Lucas Baker, Matthew Lai, Adrian Bolton, et al. Mastering the game of Go without human knowledge. *Nature*, 550(7676):354–359, 2017.

J Stolfo, Wei Fan, Wenke Lee, Andreas Prodromidis, and Philip K Chan. Cost-based modeling and evaluation for data mining with application to fraud and intrusion detection. *Results from the JAM Project by Salvatore*, pages 1–15, 2000.

TFF. TensorFlow Federated, 12 2018. URL https://github.com/tensorflow/federated.

TFP. TensorFlow Privacy, 2 2022. URL https://github.com/tensorflow/privacy.

Pauli Virtanen, Ralf Gommers, Travis E Oliphant, Matt Haberland, Tyler Reddy, David Cournapeau, Evgeni Burovski, Pearu Peterson, Warren Weckesser, Jonathan Bright, et al. SciPy 1.0: Fundamental algorithms for scientific computing in python. *Nature Methods*, 17(3):261–272, 2020.

Paul Voigt and Axel Von dem Bussche. The EU general data protection regulation (GDPR). *A Practical Guide*, 1st Ed., Springer International Publishing, Cham, 10(3152676):10–5555, 2017.

Shengjie Xu, Yi Qian, and Rose Qingyang Hu. A data-driven preprocessing scheme on anomaly detection in big data applications. In *2017 IEEE Conference on Computer Communications Workshops (INFOCOM WKSHPS)*, pages 814–819. IEEE, 2017.

Shengjie Xu, Yi Qian, and Rose Qingyang Hu. Data-driven network intelligence for anomaly detection. *IEEE Network*, 33(3):88–95, 2019a.

Shengjie Xu, Yi Qian, and Rose Qingyang Hu. A semi-supervised learning approach for network anomaly detection in fog computing. In *2019 IEEE International Conference on Communications (ICC)*, pages 1–6. IEEE, 2019b.

Shengjie Xu, Yi Qian, and Rose Qingyang Hu. Data-driven edge intelligence for robust network anomaly detection. *IEEE Transactions on Network Science and Engineering*, 7(3):1481–1492, 2019c.

Shengjie Xu, Yi Qian, and Rose Qingyang Hu. Edge intelligence assisted gateway defense in cyber security. *IEEE Network*, 34(4):14–19, 2020.

Xiaoyong Yuan, Pan He, Qile Zhu, and Xiaolin Li. Adversarial examples: Attacks and defenses for deep learning. *IEEE Transactions on Neural Networks and Learning Systems*, 30(9):2805–2824, 2019.

Alexander Ziller, Andrew Trask, Antonio Lopardo, Benjamin Szymkow, Bobby Wagner, Emma Bluemke, Jean-Mickael Nounahon, Jonathan Passerat-Palmbach, Kritika Prakash, Nick Rose, et al. PySyft: A library for easy federated learning. In *Federated Learning Systems* (eds. Muhammad Habib ur Rehman, Mohamed Medhat Gaber), pages 111–139. Springer, 2021.

Deqing Zou, Yawei Zhu, Shouhuai Xu, Zhen Li, Hai Jin, and Hengkai Ye. Interpreting deep learning-based vulnerability detector predictions based on heuristic searching. *ACM Transactions on Software Engineering and Methodology (TOSEM)*, 30(2):1–31, 2021.

2

Cyber Threats and Gateway Defense

Advanced persistent threat (APT), cyber intrusions, and malware have been maliciously disturbing the networking systems and communication networks, causing the discontinuity of assured services and further destroying critical networking devices and cyberinfrastructure. In this chapter, these cyber threats and their challenges are introduced, followed by multiple effective gateway defense methods against cyber threats. Lastly, a research study that innovates reinforcement learning for penetration test is presented.

2.1 Cyber Threats

Cyber threats refer to any possible forms of malicious attacks that seek to disrupt normal operations, access sensitive data unlawfully, or compromise any legitimate information systems. In previous research studies (Xu et al., 2019a,b, 2020), the authors summarized a few noteworthy cyber threats, which are described in the following sections.

2.1.1 Cyber Intrusions

Cyber intrusions are commonly launched by adversaries commanding several compromised machines. These intrusions are capable of causing computing and networking systems unavailable to respond to normal service requests. In Iglesias and Zseby (2015), the authors presented a comprehensive study on the traffic features, which are analyzed to explain the causes of major cyber intrusions.

In Xu et al. (2019a,b), the authors summarized the traffic features from two popular intrusion detection datasets (Revathi and Malathi, 2013; Moustafa and Slay, 2016). These features can be categorized into *basic*,

Cybersecurity in Intelligent Networking Systems, First Edition.
Shengjie Xu, Yi Qian, and Rose Qingyang Hu.
© 2023 John Wiley & Sons Ltd. Published 2023 by John Wiley & Sons Ltd.

Table 2.1 Traffic features from NSL KDD data.

Basic (individual TCP connections)	Content (within a connection suggested by domain knowledge)	Traffic (in a two-second time window)
Duration of the connection, type of protocol, network service, packet payload, status of the connection	Number of: failed login attempts, "compromised" conditions, "root" access, file creation operations, shell prompts, operations on access control files, outbound commands	Number of: connections, services, percentage of connections: with "SYN" and "REJ" errors, with the same and different services

Source: Adapted from Revathi and Malathi (2013).

content, and *traffic*. Category *basic* is composed of packet headers of discovered packets. Some of them need to be inspected from header fields and reported by flow measurements on routers, while others are kept from the connection status. Category *content* mainly consists of the packet payload, where additional data pre-processing work is required. Category *traffic* contains different characteristics of previous connections. The descriptions on the traffic features are presented in Tables 2.1 and 2.2.

As discussed by the authors in Sung and Mukkamala (2003) and Kayacik et al. (2005), information gain approach is adopted to perform an analysis on feature relevancy. The most significant features that cause an anomaly are traffic payload from source to destination, traffic payload from destination to source, and the percentage of connections to different services. Authors in Sung and Mukkamala (2003) further mentioned that the identified features offered remarkable performance in terms of computational overhead during the training process in a machine learning task.

Table 2.2 Traffic features from UNSW-NB15 data.

Flow (identifier features between hosts)	Basic (protocol connections)	Content (features of TCP/IP)	Time
Sockets information (IP address and port number), protocol type	Network service, packet payload, time-to-live (TTL)	HTTP services, mean of flow packet size	Arrival time between packets, start/end packet time, round trip time of TCP

Source: Adapted from Moustafa and Slay (2016).

In Buczak and Guven (2016), the authors discussed the types of common intrusions from the NSL KDD intrusion detection dataset. The authors summarized four main types: *Denial of Service (DoS) attacks*, such as the SYN flood attack; *Scanning or Probing attacks (Probing)*, such as surveillance and port scanning; *Remote-to-Local (R2L)* attacks, such as guessing password to unauthorized access from a remote machine; and *User-to-Root (U2R) attacks*, such as buffer overflow attack to unauthorized access to local super user (root) privileges. In Moustafa and Slay (2016), the authors offered the types of intrusions from a different perspective. The identified cyber intrusions can all be categorized into the four categories.

2.1.2 Distributed Denial of Services Attack

Distributed Denial-of-Services (DDoS) is a type of vicious and large-scale cyber threat against the system availability. Adversaries usually control a large group of infected devices to form botnets and then use these botnets to flood superfluous information and damage critical networking systems. In Xu et al. (2019a), the authors discussed a documented DDoS attack in early 2018, when the attack peak reached at 1.35 Tbps, and the traffic was flooded to compromise the developer repository site GitHub. As the botnets consist of massive infected end devices, it is critical to perform active firewall and access control schemes at edge networks to prevent DDoS attacks.

2.1.3 Malware and Shellcode

A malware is a piece of malicious software that infects a computer and disrupts its normal functions. Modern malware can take many forms. It can be embedded in document macros, run as shellcode, and much more. Malware is also versatile in the taskings it can complete. In Sun et al. (2017), the authors discussed the severity of popularization of malware. It is reported that every four seconds, a new malware program is generated. A specific type of malware may exist in over 50 variants, and the end devices where malware programs target to host are very diverse. Those facts show that effective detection over all types of malware is complex and challenging.

In Ahmed and Xu (2022), the authors presented the current state of shellcode and then proposed approaches to increase the detection rate of unknown malware. The article states that a shellcode is a sequence of machine code usually written in assembly language to perform malicious tasks on any system. These shellcodes could be injected into a vulnerable running process or added to malware and then executed as part of it.

2.2 Gateway Defense Approaches

It is crucial to secure the network gateway and defend the edge network against malicious invasions. In Xu et al. (2020), the authors described a list of defense approaches at network gateway.

2.2.1 Network Access Control

Network access control should be enforced in an edge network so that the end device connecting to a specific domain can be identified. More importantly, a customized policy should take both security and privacy into account. This new policy can be based on the basic information of the device, its current user profile, the service it requests, the resource it shares, and the timestamps of the ongoing services. Meanwhile, it is critical to strictly follow this policy, so that any new or abrupt change to that device will not be ignored.

2.2.2 Anomaly Isolation

Once a customized policy is established at the device side, it is important to group the devices into a specific network cluster so that a monitoring process will be carried out to prevent the device accessing unauthorized resources. When any misbehavior occurs inside of the network cluster, the isolation mechanism can be executed toward the devices.

2.2.3 Collaborative Learning

In intrusion detection, a high degree of latency in response would cause serious unavailability in critical online systems. A group of gateway nodes can be teamed together to collaboratively deliver more benefits and functionalities, such as forming swarm intelligence and enhancing system redundancy. The collaborative machine learning for distributed cybersecurity is presented in Figure 2.1.

While collaborative learning for gateway defense brings effective and reliable services, the security model of each participating node in the network should be examined. Any forms of physical tampering toward a trusted commanding node for learning may result in a total disruption of an access network so that malicious attacks such as data poisoning attack and model poisoning attack can be avoided.

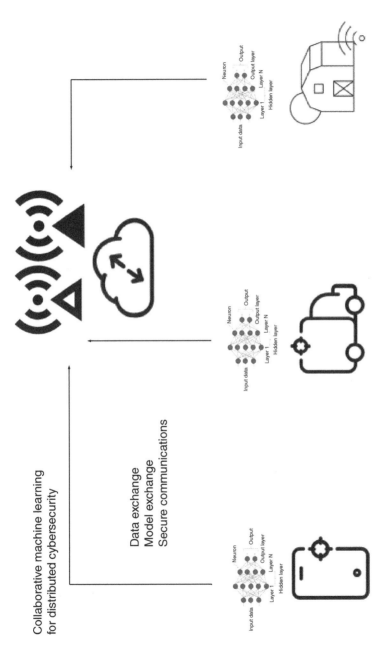

Figure 2.1 Collaborative machine learning for distributed cybersecurity.

2.2.4 Secure Local Data Learning

The traditional procedure for big data applications involves large sensitive data aggregation at the front end, pre-processing for anonymization by an edge node or a cloud node, and finally the cyber analytics. During this procedure, the varying data ownership and unauthorized permissions can cause serious privacy violations. Meanwhile, reverse engineering may also be performed to recover sensitive information. Facing these challenges, secure local data learning schemes can enable cyber analytics in a privacy-preserving way, by downloading the initial learning models from the server, then performing learning schemes locally, and finally simply sharing only the learning weights back to the cloud. The sensitive data will remain stored on the devices, and the user privacy is not compromised during the learning process. Federated learning and its use with differential privacy will be discussed more in later chapters.

2.3 Emerging Data-driven Methods for Gateway Defense

Machine learning models for gateway defense are widely discussed in the current literature, especially intrusion detection (Xu et al., 2019b). In this section, some other emerging data-driven methods are presented.

2.3.1 Semi-supervised Learning for Intrusion Detection

Semi-supervised learning is a special format of machine learning. The motivation is about the challenge to acquire the fully labeled dependent variable y. In Khan and Madden (2014), one-class classification (OCC) was introduced as a representative approach in the semi-supervised learning. Specifically, the authors emphasized a point of building semi-supervised classifiers when the negative class is either vacant, poorly sampled, or not clearly stated in a collected data source.

In most intrusion detection cases, the acquired data might comprise too much unlabeled traffic data and not too much anomalous traffic data. This shows that both supervised and unsupervised learning approaches may become infeasible to apply. Alternatively, training semi-supervised learning models on this type of traffic data would provide an effective detection on general intrusions and some specific intrusion types.

Positive and unlabeled learning (PU learning) is another representative approach in semi-supervised learning. It focuses on training a binary classifier from only positive and unlabeled sample data. Recently, the authors in Zhang et al. (2018) proposed a PU learning enabled system for potential anomalous behavior detection and provided a two-stage strategy and a cost-sensitive strategy to obtain an optimal PU learning model for anomaly detection. In Sun et al. (2017), the authors proposed a PU learning-enabled malware detection to eliminate outliers and contaminants from data.

2.3.2 Transfer Learning for Intrusion Detection

Transfer learning is a powerful machine learning paradigm that offers users with few available data to quickly build accurate learning models by "learning" from pre-trained models from large datasets. Following this approach, transfer learning can be utilized to establish a learning model efficiently, and this will greatly reduce the training overhead. Transfer learning is more suitable for applications with data scarcity scenarios as it is effective to tackle anomaly detection problems in new and unknown cyber threats when not too much labeling information is available.

In Zhao et al. (2017), the authors investigated a scenario that the performance of machine learning models was affected by the different distributions of features in the training and testing samples and the expensive overhead to generate all the labeling information. The authors proposed a feature-based transfer learning scheme to detect previously unseen cyber intrusions. The proposed approach was applied to find a learning representation that expresses a common latent subspace for different data distributions, and it was further evaluated on popular learning models.

2.3.3 Federated Learning for Privacy Preservation

Federated learning is growing rapidly in intelligent networking systems that have strong requirements for privacy protection. In Yang et al. (2019), the authors discussed that privacy-preserving decentralized collaborative machine learning could be considered as a practical solution for privacy protection in edge networks. Federated learning offers applications at the edge to train learning models on several end devices, then upload the models to the edge node for averaging a global model, and finally provide feedback from the new global model back to each device. No local data are revealed or shared to the edge node from the end devices or end users during the entire learning process.

Using this approach, challenging issues such as heavy communication overhead and large energy consumption will be alleviated. The only communication overhead existed during the learning process is the size of model parameters, and its communication overhead is far less than the data that was supposed to be uploaded to a server.

In Bonawitz et al. (2017), the authors presented a protocol involving secure data aggregation while the privacy of clients' inputs was ensured. It was evaluated in an edge network setting by aggregating user-provided model updates in a deep learning model. The security analysis was conducted in honest-but-curious and active adversary settings, and the proof showed that security was maintained when random groups of users failed.

2.3.4 Reinforcement Learning for Penetration Test

Predicting cyberattacks to networks is an ever-present challenge in the gateway defense domain. The rapid growth of AI has made this even more challenging as machine learning algorithms are now used to attack such systems while defense systems continue to protect them with traditional approaches.

Penetration test is a process about vulnerability identification, exploitation, and assessment. As one of the key methods used by organizations to strengthen the defense of their systems against cyber threats, penetration test assesses and evaluates the security of digital assets by planning, generating, and executing all possible attacks that can exploit the existing vulnerabilities (Ghanem and Chen, 2018). With increasing cyberattacks, penetration test is becoming even more crucial and troublesome at the same time, manifesting the need for intelligent approaches to innovate traditional penetration test.

Traditional penetration test prevents security breaches by mimicking black hat hackers to expose possible exploits and vulnerabilities. However, the use of these approaches is more resource and time consuming with high chances of human error caused by repetitive tasks. Using trained machine learning agents to automate this process is an important research area that still needs to be conducted. The need for real-time identification of exploitable vulnerabilities adds to the number of potential research challenges and opportunities in modern AI.

2.4 Case Study: Reinforcement Learning for Automated Post-breach Penetration Test

In this research (Chaudhary et al., 2020), the objective is to apply machine learning in the post-exploitation phase of penetration test to assess the vulnerability of the system and hence contribute to the automation process of penetration test. The agent can be trained using reinforcement learning by providing an appropriate environment to explore a compromised network and find sensitive files. By utilizing several different network environments during training, this direction can generalize agents as much as possible, allowing for more widespread application. This study discusses the limitations of current penetration test practices and the need of automation mechanisms in such tradition. A research idea is proposed to automate the post-exploit phase of penetration test using reinforcement learning, and the current environment for training the agent is described.

2.4.1 Literature Review

Researchers have analyzed the impacts of penetration test and studied different approaches to enhance them. The ability of reinforcement learning to enable an agent to learn in an interactive environment by trial-and-error approach using feedback from its own actions and experiences makes it more suitable for this study than other machine learning models.

In McKinnel et al. (2019), the authors conducted research on vulnerability assessment and pointed out different methods used for those studies and a comparison among them. They also presented potential research directions in using AI for penetration test. In Ghanem and Chen (2018), the authors proposed a hypothesis that reinforcement learning could be used to enhance penetration test. They modeled a system using partially observable Markov Decision Process (POMDP) and asserted that this approach allowed intelligent and autonomous penetration test. Researchers also proposed a general framework using deep Q-network to evade antimalware engines (Fang et al., 2019b).

Despite the use of automated tools, the current practice in penetration test is becoming complex, repetitive, and resource consuming (Ghanem and Chen, 2018). Deep Exploit, a tool using Metasploit framework, also works as a fully automated penetration test tool. However, it is not fully automated for a complete penetration test. At the post-exploitation phase of penetration test, there is still a huge gap to cover with machine learning algorithms. There are few studies using reinforcement learning for the automation in the post-breach penetration test, which makes this research novel.

2.4.2 Research Idea

Reinforcement learning analyzes actions taken by a software agent in an environment in order to maximize a reward. Figure 2.2 presents the general workflow of reinforcement learning. In recent years, methods using deep Q-learning networks have been successful in human-level controlled

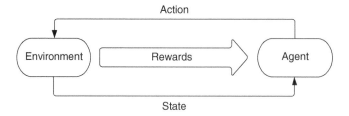

Figure 2.2 General workflow of reinforcement learning.

systems, such as game playing (Fang et al., 2019a). Because few research studies adopted reinforcement learning in the post-exploitation phase of penetration test, a model trained using deep Q-learning is proposed for the post-breach of the network.

2.4.3 Training Agent Using Deep Q-Learning

Deep Q-learning is a model-free approach that can be used for building a self-exploring agent. Figure 2.3 presents the workflow of Q-learning. The method uses neural networks to estimate Q values by feeding the initial state into the network and returning the Q-values of all possible actions as output. The Q value is calculated as

$$Q(S_t, A_t) \leftarrow Q(S_t, A_t)$$
$$+ \alpha[R_{t+1} + \gamma \max_{\alpha} Q(S_{t+1}, a) - Q(S_t, A_t)], \tag{2.1}$$

where α is the learning rate that determines the extent to which newly acquired information overrides the old one.

Q-Learning is a good candidate as the reinforcement training algorithm because of its performance when the time steps between rewards are scarce. In this study, a deep Q network is trained with TF_Agents, on top of the TensorFlow library. The trained agent will then be placed in Linux and Windows servers on virtual machines to explore compromised

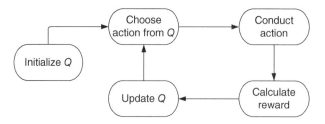

Figure 2.3 Workflow of Q-learning.

Table 2.3 Example of files granting rewards.

Server	File type	File name	User	Action
Windows	Employee information	data.csv	Admin	Exploit
Linux	Password	passwd	Admin	Exploit
Linux	Shadow	Shadow	Root	Report back the directory information

networks and find sensitive files, just as would occur during a penetration test. The training of the agent is on the modified networks. The dataset is the files over those networks such as password, shadows, configurations, and more, as shown in Table 2.3. Based on the exploration and exploitation performance of the agent, scores will be provided as reward in order to train the agent.

The actions available to the agent are a finite set of terminal commands, with placeholders that are taken from the environment. An example command is

> **cd** [placeholder]

Here, the placeholder is a file directory scanned from the current environment. Using a softmax function for the neural net output, actions to take based on maximized Q-value estimates can be determined while still allowing for agent exploration.

2.5 Summary

In this chapter, the discussions on cyber threats and their challenges are presented. By utilizing emerging data-driven methods, gateway defense can be boosted to prevent the edge network from cyber threats. A case study is presented to show the research direction on applying reinforcement learning for automated post-breach penetration test.

References

Tarek Ahmed and Shengjie Xu. Shellcoding: Hunting for Kernel32 base address. In *IEEE INFOCOM 2022-IEEE Conference on Computer Communications Workshops (INFOCOM WKSHPS)*, pages 1–2. IEEE, 2022.

Keith Bonawitz, Vladimir Ivanov, Ben Kreuter, Antonio Marcedone, H Brendan McMahan, Sarvar Patel, Daniel Ramage, Aaron Segal, and Karn Seth. Practical secure aggregation for privacy-preserving machine learning. In *Proceedings of the 2017 ACM SIGSAC Conference on Computer and Communications Security*, pages 1175–1191, 2017.

Anna L Buczak and Erhan Guven. A survey of data mining and machine learning methods for cyber security intrusion detection. *IEEE Communication Surveys and Tutorials*, 18(2):1153–1176, 2016.

Sujita Chaudhary, Austin O'Brien, and Shengjie Xu. Automated post-breach penetration testing through reinforcement learning. In *2020 IEEE Conference on Communications and Network Security (CNS)*, pages 1–2. IEEE, 2020.

Zhiyang Fang, Junfeng Wang, Jiaxuan Geng, and Xuan Kan. Feature selection for malware detection based on reinforcement learning. *IEEE Access*, 7:176177–176187, 2019a.

Zhiyang Fang, Junfeng Wang, Boya Li, Siqi Wu, Yingjie Zhou, and Haiying Huang. Evading anti-malware engines with deep reinforcement learning. *IEEE Access*, 7:48867–48879, 2019b.

Mohamed C Ghanem and Thomas M Chen. Reinforcement learning for intelligent penetration testing. In *2018 Second World Conference on Smart Trends in Systems, Security and Sustainability (WorldS4)*, pages 185–192. IEEE, 2018.

Félix Iglesias and Tanja Zseby. Analysis of network traffic features for anomaly detection. *Machine Learning*, 101(1–3):59–84, 2015.

H Günes Kayacik, A Nur Zincir-Heywood, and Malcolm I Heywood. Selecting features for intrusion detection: A feature relevance analysis on KDD'99 intrusion detection datasets. In *Proceedings of the Third Annual Conference on Privacy, Security and Trust*, volume 94, pages 1723–1722, 2005.

Shehroz S Khan and Michael G Madden. One-class classification: Taxonomy of study and review of techniques. *The Knowledge Engineering Review*, 29(3):345–374, 2014.

Dean Richard McKinnel, Tooska Dargahi, Ali Dehghantanha, and Kim-Kwang Raymond Choo. A systematic literature review and meta-analysis on artificial intelligence in penetration testing and vulnerability assessment. *Computers and Electrical Engineering*, 75:175–188, 2019.

Nour Moustafa and Jill Slay. The evaluation of network anomaly detection systems: Statistical analysis of the UNSW-NB15 data set and the comparison with the KDD99 data set. *Information Security Journal: A Global Perspective*, 25(1–3):18–31, 2016.

S Revathi and A Malathi. A detailed analysis on NSL-KDD dataset using various machine learning techniques for intrusion detection. *International*

Journal of Engineering Research & Technology (IJERT), 2(12):1848–1853, 2013.

Lichao Sun, Xiaokai Wei, Jiawei Zhang, Lifang He, S Yu Philip, and Witawas Srisa-an. Contaminant removal for android malware detection systems. In *2017 IEEE International Conference on Big Data (Big Data)*, pages 1053–1062. IEEE, 2017.

Andrew H Sung and Srinivas Mukkamala. Identifying important features for intrusion detection using support vector machines and neural networks. In *2003 Symposium on Applications and the Internet, 2003. Proceedings.*, pages 209–216. IEEE, 2003.

Shengjie Xu, Yi Qian, and Rose Qingyang Hu. Data-driven network intelligence for anomaly detection. *IEEE Network*, 33(3):88–95, 2019a.

Shengjie Xu, Yi Qian, and Rose Qingyang Hu. Data-driven edge intelligence for robust network anomaly detection. *IEEE Transactions on Network Science and Engineering*, 7(3):1481–1492, 2019b.

Shengjie Xu, Yi Qian, and Rose Qingyang Hu. Edge intelligence assisted gateway defense in cyber security. *IEEE Network*, 34(4):14–19, 2020.

Qiang Yang, Yang Liu, Tianjian Chen, and Yongxin Tong. Federated machine learning: Concept and applications. *ACM Transactions on Intelligent Systems and Technology (TIST)*, 10(2):1–19, 2019.

Ya-Lin Zhang, Longfei Li, Jun Zhou, Xiaolong Li, and Zhi-Hua Zhou. Anomaly detection with partially observed anomalies. In *Companion of the The Web Conference 2018 on The Web Conference 2018*, pages 639–646. International World Wide Web Conferences Steering Committee, 2018.

Juan Zhao, Sachin Shetty, and Jan Wei Pan. Feature-based transfer learning for network security. In *MILCOM 2017-2017 IEEE Military Communications Conference (MILCOM)*, pages 17–22. IEEE, 2017.

3

Edge Computing and Secure Edge Intelligence

Edge computing (Sun and Ansari, 2016) has been envisioned as an enabling technology to support data-driven services and local Internet of Things (IoT) applications by pushing computing, storage, and networking resources from the cloud to the network edge. In this chapter, edge computing is presented to highlight its key advances and unique capabilities in communication networks. The concept of secure edge intelligence is then introduced.

3.1   Edge Computing

In Bonomi et al. (2012), the authors from Cisco Systems defined edge computing as "a paradigm that extends the computing, storage, and service to the edge of the network." Although the integration of cloud computing and end devices has addressed some problems, centralization of resources in cloud computing remains a huge gap among end devices and the cloud. This inevitably increases a huge communication delay and overhead. Edge computing does not replace cloud computing for remote data computation, storage, and processing but facilitates a new and scalable hierarchical architecture. Compared to cloud computing, an intelligence system enabled by edge computing can provide significant benefits, such as low communication latency and long-term cost-effectiveness.

As the rapid development of modern communication technologies, artificial intelligence, and the revolution of computing devices, edge computing inevitably becomes the core direction in major smart applications. A system model using edge computing is presented in Figure 3.1. While cloud computing provides strong and powerful computation, storage, and networking services, edge computing offers more advantages in specific application-aware services. In recent studies (Xu et al., 2019b, 2020), the following aspects justify the need for effective edge computing.

Cybersecurity in Intelligent Networking Systems, First Edition.
Shengjie Xu, Yi Qian, and Rose Qingyang Hu.
© 2023 John Wiley & Sons Ltd. Published 2023 by John Wiley & Sons Ltd.

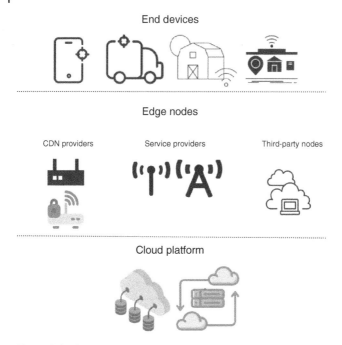

Figure 3.1 A system model provided with edge computing.

First, the need for edge computing is based on large data acquisition and aggregation at the user end. The legacy mode for obtaining and aggregating data follows a high-cost and low-efficiency pattern. In an example, it is estimated that the total installed base of IoT-connected devices is projected to amount to 75.44 billion worldwide by 2025 (Sun and Ansari, 2016). It will be an impractical and inappropriate idea to collect and aggregate the data by a centralized node in an ineffective and coarse way.

Second, the need is affected by various communication scenarios that require continuous and real-time requirements. The traditional mode for those scenarios follows an acknowledge-response approach, in which data are uploaded pending for processing and commands are then issued from a remote central node. Such an approach always produces a huge amount of communication and computational overhead. For instance, self-driving vehicle applications will not tolerate such a high latency if that approach is followed.

Third, the need is impacted by services that require high system availability and robust assurance. If a central system suffers from a failure caused by malicious cyberattacks or the disruption of communication networks, the availability of a guaranteed service will be compromised. For instance, content delivery network (CDN) providers can offer various services for end users. If all the demanded and guaranteed services are interrupted and disrupted, then the quality of experience (QoE) (Ong et al., 2003; Zhang et al., 2015) from end users will decrease and the market share will shrink. In addition, huge economic losses will be faced by large corporations that rely on CDN providers to broadcast their services.

Edge computing can be a solution to tackle the existing and upcoming challenges, especially the ones in cybersecurity (Ni et al., 2019). By utilizing edge computing, a fully functioning cyberinfrastructure can expedite the evolution of intrusion detection by providing parallel virtual machines and advanced processing units for computing, deploying distributed big data framework for real-time data streaming and storage, and establishing dedicated network channels for peer collaborations and further transfer the trained model to adjacent edge computing nodes (Pan and Yang, 2010; Yang et al., 2007). In the task of intrusion detection, large amounts of latency will cause severe unavailability in critical online systems. Meanwhile, cyberattacks will be continuously carried out by adversaries. With edge computing, a group of edge computing nodes can be teamed together to build joint secure solutions, such as forming collaborative intelligence for cybersecurity and enhancing system redundancy.

3.2 Key Advances in Edge Computing

There are a few representative articles that provided contributions in edge computing for communication networks. Here, these advances are summarized in terms of security, reliability, and survivability.

3.2.1 Security

There are several research articles focusing on advancing the security by enabling edge computing. In Chen et al. (2014), the authors presented an adaptive IoT trust protocol for service-oriented architecture-based IoT systems with applications in service composition. Specifically, the authors designed an adaptive and scalable trust management protocol and developed a distributed collaborative filtering technique to select trust feedback from owners of IoT nodes sharing similar social interests. In Chandrasekhar and Singhal (2015), the authors proposed a query authentication scheme for cloud-based storage system where the data were populated by multiple sources and retrieved by the clients. The proposed scheme focused on the identity confirmation in cloud-based or ad hoc networks. In Jiang et al. (2016), the authors proposed an untraceable two-factor authentication scheme based on elliptic curve cryptography for wireless sensor network-based IoT applications. In Hu et al. (2017), a security and privacy preservation scheme for edge computing-based face identification and resolution framework in IoT was proposed. Specifically, the identity authentication scheme, data encryption scheme, and data integrity checking scheme were proposed to meet the demands of confidentiality, integrity, and availability in the processes of face identification and face resolution.

In Li et al. (2017), the authors introduced a feasible attack model in an IoT fog architecture and implemented attack demonstrations to show the severe consequences of such attacks. Additionally, the authors proposed a lightweight countermeasure using Bloom filters to monitor stealthy packet modifications. In Zhou et al. (2014), an authorized accessible privacy model and a patient self-controllable multi-level privacy-preserving cooperative authentication scheme realizing three different levels of security and privacy requirement in the distributed m-healthcare cloud computing system were proposed. In Salonikias et al. (2015), the authors studied the operational characteristics of a proposed paradigm utilizing edge computing and identified corresponding access control issues. To address these issues in such a versatile and highly distributed environment, the authors presented the key pointers of an attribute-based access control scheme suitable for edge computing. In Zhang et al. (2018), the authors proposed a method based on edge computing that performs most computations at terminal (mobile devices). Specifically, a lightweight and fast response method for mobile devices to detect spammers in mobile social networks was introduced. This scheme leads to a better real-time performance and adapts to the wide geographical distribution and the high mobility of mobile devices.

In Arshad et al. (2011), the authors introduced an abstract model for integrated intrusion detection and severity analysis for cloud for facilitating minimal intrusion response time while preserving the overall security of the cloud infrastructures. In Sanjay Ram (2012), the authors discussed the mutual and reliable security of cloud computing. Specifically, the authors proposed a method to build a mutual and reliable computing environment for the cloud computing system by integrating the trusted computing platform into the cloud computing system and paying attention to the security requirements in the cloud computing environment. In Liu et al. (2018b), the authors discussed the existing challenges of intelligent traffic light control systems and proposed two secure intelligent traffic light control schemes using edge computing to cope with those challenges. In Park et al. (2013), the authors also proposed certificate mechanisms for preventing the Sybil attack in a vehicular ad hoc network. Specifically, the authors focused on an early-stage vehicular ad hoc network (VANET) when the number of smart vehicles is only a small fraction of the vehicles on the road and the only infrastructure components available are the roadside units. In Wang et al. (2011), the authors discussed the new security risks toward the correctness of data in clouds. Based on the discussion, the authors proposed a flexible distributed storage integrity auditing mechanism, utilizing the homomorphic token and distributed erasure-coded data to address this problem and further achieve a secure and dependable cloud storage service. In Li et al. (2012), the authors studied the patient-centric, secure sharing of personal health records stored on semi-trusted servers and focused on addressing the complicated and challenging key management issues. Based on this objective, the authors proposed a novel attribute-based encryption (ABE)-based framework for patient-centric secure sharing of personal health records in cloud computing environments under the multi-owner settings.

3.2.2 Reliability

There are several research articles focusing on advancing the reliability by enabling edge computing. In Araújo et al. (2017), the authors developed a smart parking system able to gather quantitative information and provided them through an extensible platform to drivers and other smart city applications. This work aims to evaluate the reliability of smart parking through an empirical analysis of how many errors occur in a certain time window, the success and error rates, and the most common kind of error produced. In Lyu et al. (2018), the authors presented a novel three-layer integration architecture including the cloud, edge computing, and Internet of Things, and they proposed a lightweight request and admission framework to resolve the scalability problem. Following the proposed framework, a selective offloading scheme was developed to minimize the energy consumption of the IoT devices and further reduce the signaling overhead of edge computing.

In Liu and Zhang (2018), the authors proposed a scheme to address the offloading computation task to multiple edge nodes for 5G network in an efficient and reliable way. The offloading scheme considers both computations and communications of the task and jointly optimizes the latency and reliability in mobile edge computing. In Liu et al. (2018a), the authors achieved the optimal holistic edge computing performance for IoT reducing total energy consumption and total execution time and improving the system reliability and mobile users' QoE. A tensor-based holistic edge computing optimization framework for IoT was presented to address this problem. In Lorenzo et al. (2018), the authors presented a novel design of a robust dynamic edge network architecture for IoT which leverages the latest advances of mobile devices to dynamically harvest unused resources and mitigate network congestion. The proposed design provides solutions at the physical, access, networking, application, and business layers to improve network robustness.

3.2.3 Survivability

There are several research articles focusing on advancing survivability by enabling edge computing. In Peng et al. (2018), a survivable network planning model based on software-defined networking for software-defined data center networks in smart city was presented. Authors developed a data center network planning based on big data for rational deployment and interconnection of network infrastructures, which can improve the network survivability and flexibility of edge-assisted IoT networks. In Modarresi and Sterbenz (2017), the authors explained how the edge computing architecture improves network resilience by providing autonomy through the local processing to the edge network. Various network simulations to study network traffic with and without an edge layer were conducted to test load balancing among edge nodes at the edge.

In Modarresi et al. (2017), a framework of edge computing can be extended to install any service of choice is defined for improving network resilience using software-defined networking (SDN) and edge nodes. The framework utilizes edge nodes that are attached to OpenFlow switches and have the ability to inspect data packets that pass through the network. In Colman-Meixner et al. (2016), the authors surveyed an overall summary of cloud resiliency approaches and a short analysis of major trends and open problems in edge computing and cloud computing resiliency.

3.3   Secure Edge Intelligence

For critical information and communication technology (ICT) platforms that deliver assured online services, an intelligent cyber defense system against anomalous events and malicious threats is of great importance. Various cyberattacks were launched targeting critical online services, such as e-commerce, e-health, social networking, and other major cyber applications, whose service availability and information security have been viciously threatened. In one article (Rothrock et al., 2018), the authors indicated that a cyberattack that caused a massive data breach at the credit reporting agency Equifax Inc. had affected nearly 143 million U.S. consumers, making it the headline news of cybersecurity in 2017. In future cyberspaces, the failure of performing an intelligent cyber defense system will lead to disastrous collapses of information confidentiality, data integrity, and service availability in an unpredictable way (Xu et al., 2019).

Nowadays, cyberattacks can be launched by threat actors and adversarial attackers who maliciously control massive end devices that are hosted at the network edge. In this scenario, end devices will go through the edge network to flood networking traffic. The primary objective of this research (Xu et al., 2019) is to design a secure and robust edge intelligence so that assured and reliable services can be guaranteed and uninterrupted.

3.3.1 Background and Motivation

Secure edge intelligence plays a vital role in identifying any unauthorized access, malicious alteration, and destruction of critical ICT systems. Traditionally, the rule-based and signature-based strategies were applied for cybersecurity tasks such as intrusion detection (Yu et al., 2012). As the amount of network traffic increases, these strategies will produce more and more Type I and Type II errors, making them ineffective to detect new types of cyber threats. In the past few years, the intrusion detection system has rapidly evolved from traditional rule-based decision-making configurations to modern intelligent solutions.

In Buczak and Guven (2016), the authors provided a comprehensive study on applying data-driven approaches and other statistical methods to detect anomalous cases. This study offers a promising direction for the design of secure edge intelligence. The authors described a framework of three phases to detect anomalous behaviors using machine learning models. The first phase contains three steps, including identifying the key features of training data, selecting a subset of necessary features for classification tasks, and learning a model using training data. The second phase is for validation by selecting an optimal learning model reflected on validation data. The third phase is for testing by deploying the optimal model for classifying unknown data. The discussed framework provides a general presentation of intelligent detection over cyber intrusions. Because of the richness of machine learning models, the authors indicated that it is hard to make a recommendation for each method and the decision should be made by considering factors such as time to train a model, time to classify an unknown traffic package, and the understandability of the final classifier. Meanwhile, with the acquisition of more and more incoming traffic data with different patterns and new types of intrusions, the classifier should also be updated continuously. Therefore, these challenges should be addressed in the secure edge intelligence.

The traditional intrusion detection system is based on a singular machine deployed in the gateway of a closed network. In this case, a detection system may be isolated from the outside world as this machine will get familiar with the known attacks based on the learning model it trains. However, the system will become vulnerable when it encounters unknown threats and even new types of attacks that are launched coordinately. To tackle these challenges, the authors in Folino and Sabatino (2016) highlighted the distribution of the computational load using virtual environments. The authors in Moustafa et al. (2018) pointed out that most intrusion detection systems can be applicable for secure edge intelligence to detect malicious activities because of the decentralized architecture, high scalable deployment, and powerful computation, storage, and networking services.

3.3.2   Design of Detection Module

In secure edge intelligence, the detection module should be designed to follow the basic learning workflow while avoiding common pitfalls discussed in Chapter 1. As suggested by Ahmed et al. (2016), three modules are illustrated in the detection module of secure edge intelligence.

3.3.2.1   Data Pre-processing

The collected traffic data are usually in an unstructured format; thus, effective data cleaning on categorical values and robust data scaling on numerical values are needed. Once data pre-processing is finished, cleaned data that consist of original features are ready for model learning.

Although original features of traffic data can be applied directly to identify cyber intrusions, feature selection has received growing attention. By performing feature selection methods, anomalous data will become transformed data with most redundant features eliminated, while the majority information of the original data are still preserved.

3.3.2.2   Model Learning

Supervised learning trains a learning model based on the training data and then applies f for future prediction. Given a large amount of traffic data with features X and label Y, the objective of a supervised learning model is to minimize a cost function $\mathscr{C}$ so that an optimal model could be trained to test on future incoming traffic and to predict its label Y'. During the model learning, cross-validation should be applied to build robust models that generalize well.

Training data are used for building up an initial learning model, where a model f is learned given the available training data. In this way, any input will be "paired" with an expected output. Note that in practice, multiple learning models (e.g. logistic regression (LR), decision tree (DT), artificial neural network (ANN), random forest (RF), boosting methods, support vector machine (SVM), and ensemble learning (EL)) are trained together to compare their performance during the cross-validation phase. However, there are no universal learning models that work for all detection problems.

To assess the "wellness" of participating models, a validation set is used to evaluate the trained models. Prediction results from the validation set serve as an estimation of the error rate that will be reflected in the testing set. During cross-validation, the best-fitted learning model will be chosen from the participating models. This selection is based on the metric used in the detection problem. Once the best-fitted learning model is selected, it will be applied on the test set to perform prediction over unseen traffic data.

3.3.2.3 Model Updating

Once the model is selected, it starts to predict the incoming network traffic. However, this type of model learning is obtained in a batch mode. This mode lacks the adaptability to the variety of traffic data. Such trained models should not be kept forever in secure edge intelligence as new forms of cyber threats will always target critical online systems. Learning model should be constantly updated.

In a local environment, the entire data must be available during the whole batch training. Only when training is completed, the learning model can be applied to perform prediction. The main purpose of performing online machine learning is that learning models should make predictions continuously (Nguyen and Franke, 2012). It trains data in an incremental way, and the learning model is continuously updated as more data flow into the server. With new data as input, the model weights will be adjusted to fit the new data. The authors in Xu et al. (2017) discussed the use of online machine learning for intrusion detection. The online gradient descent algorithm is commonly applied, and it performs gradient descent on a loss function until it obtains a minimum error (Hu et al., 2014).

Solely relying on isolated edge intelligence is not ideal to detect coordinated attacks. As Folino and Sabatino (2016) pointed out, one limitation in traditional intrusion detection systems is that one system will become isolated as it monitors only a small amount of a network. Additionally, an isolated intrusion detection system may be effective in detecting certain types of cyber threats, while another one is good at detecting others. This case also brings an imbalance among all edge intelligence systems.

The authors in Zhou et al. (2010) directed their attention to collaborative intrusion detection systems, which correlate information on cyberattacks originating from different networks. As discussed before, a swarm intelligence is needed for the update of the detection module globally.

3.3.3 Challenges Against Poisoning Attacks

Edge computing has been envisioned as an enabling technology to support data-driven services and local IoT applications. Although the advance of edge computing on service latency has been well studied, security on data usage in edge computing has not been clearly identified (Ni et al., 2019). Traditional centralized machine learning for edge computing was proposed to address challenges in cybersecurity, but it cannot fully support such ubiquitous deployments and applications because of infrastructure shortcomings such as limited bandwidth, intermittent network connectivity, and strict delay constraints (Li et al., 2018).

Federated learning for edge computing is becoming a practical solution. Federated learning pushes model training to the devices from which data originate emerged as a promising alternative ML paradigm (McMahan et al., 2016). Federated learning enables a multitude of participants to construct a joint machine learning model without exposing their private training data (McMahan et al., 2016; Melis et al., 2019). Although federated learning is being considered as a promising solution, a new type of cyberattacks, namely poisoning attack, has been carried out by insiders and outsiders to compromise the distributed systems at the network edge.

3.4   Summary

In this chapter, edge computing is presented to highlight its key advances and unique capabilities in edge networks. The concept of secure edge intelligence is then introduced for the future of collaborative cybersecurity platforms in the edge networks.

References

Mohiuddin Ahmed, Abdun Naser Mahmood, and Jiankun Hu. A survey of network anomaly detection techniques. *Journal of Network and Computer Applications*, 60:19–31, 2016.

Anderson Araújo, Rubem Kalebe, Gustavo Gira o, Kayo Gonçalves, Bianor Neto, et al. Reliability analysis of an IoT-based smart parking application for smart cities. In *2017 IEEE International Conference on Big Data (Big Data)*, pages 4086–4091. IEEE, 2017.

Junaid Arshad, Paul Townend, and Jie Xu. An abstract model for integrated intrusion detection and severity analysis for clouds. *International Journal of Cloud Applications and Computing (IJCAC)*, 1(1):1–16, 2011.

Flavio Bonomi, Rodolfo Milito, Jiang Zhu, and Sateesh Addepalli. Fog computing and its role in the Internet of Things. In *Proceedings of the First Edition of the MCC Workshop on Mobile Cloud Computing*, pages 13–16. ACM, 2012.

Anna L Buczak and Erhan Guven. A survey of data mining and machine learning methods for cyber security intrusion detection. *IEEE Communication Surveys and Tutorials*, 18(2):1153–1176, 2016.

Santosh Chandrasekhar and Mukesh Singhal. Efficient and scalable query authentication for cloud-based storage systems with multiple data sources. *IEEE Transactions on Services computing*, 10(4):520–533, 2015.

Ray Chen, Jia Guo, and Fenye Bao. Trust management for SOA-based IoT and its application to service composition. *IEEE Transactions on Services Computing*, 9(3):482–495, 2014.

Carlos Colman-Meixner, Chris Develder, Massimo Tornatore, and Biswanath Mukherjee. A survey on resiliency techniques in cloud computing infrastructures and applications. *IEEE Communication Surveys and Tutorials*, 18(3):2244–2281, 2016.

Gianluigi Folino and Pietro Sabatino. Ensemble based collaborative and distributed intrusion detection systems: A survey. *Journal of Network and Computer Applications*, 66:1–16, 2016.

Weiming Hu, Jun Gao, Yanguo Wang, Ou Wu, and Stephen Maybank. Online adaboost-based parameterized methods for dynamic distributed network intrusion detection. *IEEE Transactions on Cybernetics*, 44(1):66–82, 2014.

Pengfei Hu, Huansheng Ning, Tie Qiu, Houbing Song, Yanna Wang, and Xuanxia Yao. Security and privacy preservation scheme of face identification and resolution framework using fog computing in Internet of Things. *IEEE Internet of Things Journal*, 4(5):1143–1155, 2017.

Qi Jiang, Jianfeng Ma, Fushan Wei, Youliang Tian, Jian Shen, and Yuanyuan Yang. An untraceable temporal-credential-based two-factor authentication scheme using ECC for wireless sensor networks. *Journal of Network and Computer Applications*, 76:37–48, 2016.

Ming Li, Shucheng Yu, Yao Zheng, Kui Ren, and Wenjing Lou. Scalable and secure sharing of personal health records in cloud computing using attribute-based encryption. *IEEE Transactions on Parallel and Distributed Systems*, 24(1):131–143, 2012.

Cheng Li, Zhengrui Qin, Ed Novak, and Qun Li. Securing SDN infrastructure of IoT–fog networks from MitM attacks. *IEEE Internet of Things Journal*, 4(5):1156–1164, 2017.

He Li, Kaoru Ota, and Mianxiong Dong. Learning IoT in edge: Deep learning for the Internet of Things with edge computing. *IEEE Network*, 32(1):96–101, 2018.

Jianhui Liu and Qi Zhang. Offloading schemes in mobile edge computing for ultra-reliable low latency communications. *IEEE Access*, 6:12825–12837, 2018.

Huazhong Liu, Laurence T Yang, Man Lin, Dexiang Yin, and Yimu Guo. A tensor-based holistic edge computing optimization framework for Internet of Things. *IEEE Network*, 32(1):88–95, 2018a.

Jian Liu, Jiangtao Li, Lei Zhang, Feifei Dai, Yuanfei Zhang, Xinyu Meng, and Jian Shen. Secure intelligent traffic light control using fog computing. *Future Generation Computer Systems*, 78:817–824, 2018b.

Beatriz Lorenzo, Juan Garcia-Rois, Xuanheng Li, Javier Gonzalez-Castano, and Yuguang Fang. A robust dynamic edge network architecture for the Internet of Things. *IEEE Network*, 32(1):8–15, 2018.

Xinchen Lyu, Hui Tian, Li Jiang, Alexey Vinel, Sabita Maharjan, Stein Gjessing, and Yan Zhang. Selective of floading in mobile edge computing for the green Internet of Things. *IEEE Network*, 32(1):54–60, 2018.

H Brendan McMahan, Eider Moore, Daniel Ramage, and Blaise Agüera y Arcas. Federated learning of deep networks using model averaging. *arXiv preprint arXiv:1602.05629*, 2016.

Luca Melis, Congzheng Song, Emiliano De Cristofaro, and Vitaly Shmatikov. Exploiting unintended feature leakage in collaborative learning. In *2019 IEEE Symposium on Security and Privacy (SP)*, pages 691–706. IEEE, 2019.

Amir Modarresi and James P G Sterbenz. Toward resilient networks with fog computing. In *2017 9th International Workshop on Resilient Networks Design and Modeling (RNDM)*, pages 1–7. IEEE, 2017.

Amir Modarresi, Siddharth Gangadhar, and James P G Sterbenz. A framework for improving network resilience using SDN and fog nodes. In *2017 9th International Workshop on Resilient Networks Design and Modeling (RNDM)*, pages 1–7. IEEE, 2017.

Nour Moustafa, Erwin Adi, Benjamin Turnbull, and Jiankun Hu. A new threat intelligence scheme for safeguarding industry 4.0 systems. *IEEE Access*, 6:32910–32924, 2018.

Hai Thanh Nguyen and Katrin Franke. Adaptive intrusion detection system via online machine learning. In *2012 12th International Conference on Hybrid Intelligent Systems (HIS)*, pages 271–277. IEEE, 2012.

Jianbing Ni, Xiaodong Lin, and Xuemin Sherman Shen. Toward edge-assisted Internet of Things: From security and efficiency perspectives. *IEEE Network*, 33(2):50–57, 2019.

Chui Sian Ong, Klara Nahrstedt, and Wanghong Yuan. Quality of protection for mobile multimedia applications. In *2003 International Conference on Multimedia and Expo. ICME'03. Proceedings (Cat. No. 03TH8698)*, volume 2, pages II–137. IEEE, 2003.

Sinno Jialin Pan and Qiang Yang. A survey on transfer learning. *IEEE Transactions on Knowledge and Data Engineering*, 22(10):1345–1359, 2010.

Soyoung Park, Baber Aslam, Damla Turgut, and Cliff C Zou. Defense against sybil attack in the initial deployment stage of vehicular ad hoc network based on roadside unit support. *Security and Communication Networks*, 6(4):523–538, 2013.

Yuhuai Peng, Xiaojie Wang, Dawei Shen, Wei Yan, Yanhua Fu, and Qingxu Deng. Design and modeling of survivable network planning for software-defined data center networks in smart city. *International Journal of Communication Systems*, 31(16):e3509, 2018.

Ray A Rothrock, James Kaplan, and Friso Van Der Oord. The board's role in managing cybersecurity risks. *MIT Sloan Management Review*, 59(2):12–15, 2018.

Stavros Salonikias, Ioannis Mavridis, and Dimitris Gritzalis. Access control issues in utilizing fog computing for transport infrastructure. In *International Conference on Critical Information Infrastructures Security*, pages 15–26. Springer, 2015.

M Sanjay Ram. Secure cloud computing based on mutual intrusion detection system. *International Journal of Computer Application*, 1(2):57–67, 2012.

Xiang Sun and Nirwan Ansari. EdgeIoT: Mobile edge computing for the Internet of Things. *IEEE Communications Magazine*, 54(12):22–29, 2016.

Cong Wang, Qian Wang, Kui Ren, Ning Cao, and Wenjing Lou. Toward secure and dependable storage services in cloud computing. *IEEE Transactions on Services Computing*, 5(2):220–232, 2011.

Shengjie Xu, Yi Qian, and Rose Qingyang Hu. A data-driven preprocessing scheme on anomaly detection in big data applications. In *2017 IEEE Conference on Computer Communications Workshops (INFOCOM WKSHPS)*, pages 814–819. IEEE, 2017.

Shengjie Xu, Yi Qian, and Rose Qingyang Hu. Data-driven network intelligence for anomaly detection. *IEEE Network*, 33(3):88–95, 2019a.

Shengjie Xu, Yi Qian, and Rose Qingyang Hu. Data-driven edge intelligence for robust network anomaly detection. *IEEE Transactions on Network Science and Engineering*, 7(3):1481–1492, 2019b.

Shengjie Xu, Yi Qian, and Rose Qingyang Hu. Edge intelligence assisted gateway defense in cyber security. *IEEE Network*, 34(4):14–19, 2020.

Qiang Yang, Wenyuan Dai, Guirong Xue, et al. Boosting for transfer learning. In *Proceedings of the 24th International Conference on Machine Learning, Corvallis, USA*, pages 193–200, 2007.

Shui Yu, Wanlei Zhou, Weijia Jia, Song Guo, Yong Xiang, and Feilong Tang. Discriminating DDoS attacks from flash crowds using flow correlation coefficient. *IEEE Transactions on Parallel and Distributed Systems*, 23(6):1073–1080, 2012.

Kuan Zhang, Kan Yang, Xiaohui Liang, Zhou Su, Xuemin Shen, and Henry H Luo. Security and privacy for mobile healthcare networks: From a quality of protection perspective. *IEEE Wireless Communications*, 22(4):104–112, 2015.

Jiahao Zhang, Qiang Li, Xiaoqi Wang, Bo Feng, and Dong Guo. Towards fast and lightweight spam account detection in mobile social networks through fog computing. *Peer-to-Peer Networking and Applications*, 11(4):778–792, 2018.

Chenfeng Vincent Zhou, Christopher Leckie, and Shanika Karunasekera. A survey of coordinated attacks and collaborative intrusion detection. *Computers & Security*, 29(1):124–140, 2010.

Jun Zhou, Xiaodong Lin, Xiaolei Dong, and Zhenfu Cao. PSMPA: Patient self-controllable and multi-level privacy-preserving cooperative authentication in distributedm-healthcare cloud computing system. *IEEE Transactions on Parallel and Distributed Systems*, 26(6):1693–1703, 2014.

4

Edge Intelligence for Intrusion Detection

In this chapter, the research (Xu et al., 2019) on edge intelligence for intrusion detection is presented. First, the design of edge intelligence is presented. The entire architecture includes edge cyberinfrastructure, edge artificial intelligence (AI) engine, and threat intelligence. The proposed edge intelligence for intrusion detection is evaluated in terms of detection accuracy and computational efficiency.

4.1 Edge Cyberinfrastructure

Edge cyberinfrastructure acts as the supporting foundation in edge intelligence. It lies in the bottom layer, and it serves for the exchange of network traffic data seamlessly between itself and the edge AI engine. As an important characteristic of "Infrastructure as a Service (IaaS)" from cloud computing technology, edge cyberinfrastructure provides APIs to establish the underlying network infrastructure, such as physical computing resources, data partitioning, and dedicated network channels. As presented in Figure 4.1, three units in this infrastructure are highlighted to support the fundamental computing and storage services.

Parallel-based computational units are offered so that multiple virtual machines can be established to store different types of subsets that are partitioned from the original data. All the subsets will be utilized for data learning individually, and each machine provides a stable computing host. Computational engines are essential to the edge cyberinfrastructure. Central processing unit (CPU), graphics processing unit (GPU), and tensor processing unit (TPU) are the guarantee of any efficient data learning process.

A robust storage platform is provided so that different types of data can be hosted and further processed. As presented in Figure 4.2, most offline data are stored and processed in the batch mode, and it can be further

Cybersecurity in Intelligent Networking Systems, First Edition.
Shengjie Xu, Yi Qian, and Rose Qingyang Hu.
© 2023 John Wiley & Sons Ltd. Published 2023 by John Wiley & Sons Ltd.

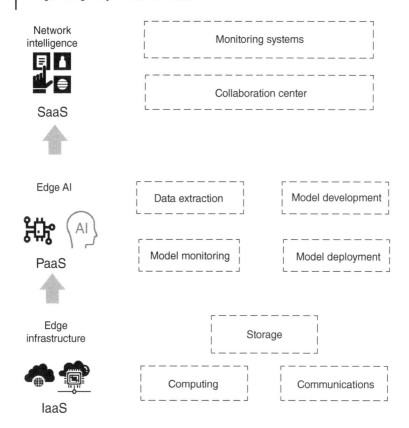

Figure 4.1 Edge intelligence for intrusion detection.

trained through a big data framework, such as *Hadoop* and *MapReduce*. For real-time applications, the data will be hosted in the streaming mode. Newly gathered data will be processed and learned through streaming-based storage platforms such as *Spark Streaming*.

Communication channels will deliver the model weights that are generated on the computing machines. The goal is to establish a dedicated channel between any trusted edge computing nodes so that the collaborative machine learning can be conducted in a secure channel without the disruption by adversaries.

4.2 Edge AI Engine

An edge AI engine is essential to data pre-processing, model learning, and predictive analytics. It lies in the middle layer. As an important characteristic

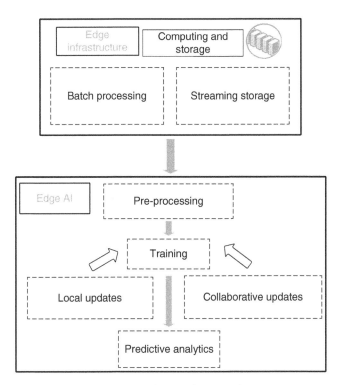

Figure 4.2 The framework of data-driven learning process.

of "Platform as a Service (PaaS)" from cloud computing technology, an edge AI engine offers a platform allowing multiple edge nodes to manage collaborative learning tasks. As presented in Figures 4.1 and 4.2, four main tasks are presented in a standard workflow, including feature engineering, model learning, model update, and predictive analytics.

4.2.1 Feature Engineering

Feature engineering utilizes domain knowledge of the referred data to create features that boost the process of data learning. In this study, the task of feature engineering focuses on dimension reduction and feature selection. By utilizing principal component analysis (PCA) for dimension reduction, most of the redundant information can be removed. In this way, the majority information is retained from the original data and the speed of data learning is improved. Feature selection works on extracting the useful information from the original dataset. Once the newly transformed data are created, a machine learning model can be trained.

4.2.2 Model Learning

Model learning aims to train a best-fitted model from a training set and a validation set. In machine learning, ensemble learning is widely utilized for data learning tasks. Ensemble learning adopts multiple learning models together to obtain a better predictive performance than an individual model alone. In this research, ensemble learning models are tested during the experimental study. In order to train an ensemble learning model, a linear combination of multiple models (e.g. logistic regression (LR), decision tree (DT), neural networks, random forest (RF), and support vector machine) are available as candidate models. In an example, a k-fold cross-validation is conducted by choosing a weight vector $w = \{w_{LR}, w_{DT}, w_{RF}\}$, from the set of vectors with entries in $\{0.1, 0.2, \ldots, 0.9\}$. In this linear combination, each model is assigned with a weight, and the sum of all weights is 100%. An edge node will create an additional parallel machine to list all the possible combinations and select the final ensemble learning model given the combination of models that provides the best value in metrics. Meanwhile, the weight vector of each model will be recorded. After finalizing the weight vector, the edge node will compare the final ensemble learning model with three independent models and then select the final local learning model.

Training a best-fitted model from scratch at each edge node consumes huge time and computing resources. Transfer learning has emerged as a new learning paradigm to address this problem. It is used to apply the pre-trained model from edge node A to edge node B. In practice, transfer learning enables the learning model trained from an edge node to be planted into its trusted adjacent node, while the performance robustness of the model is still guaranteed. In other studies, federated learning (Smith et al., 2017; Brisimi et al., 2018) also becomes effective for global learning.

4.2.3 Model Update

Because of the rapid changes in the cyber environment, learning models should be constantly updated to face new types of cyber threats and unknown attacks. In this step, model updating is performed from two aspects.

For a single edge node, online machine learning approaches will be adopted to continuously make intrusion detection even when the model is still learning. As long as the incoming network traffic flows in, the parameters of the local learning model will be adjusted to perceive the new types of network traffic. For a group of trusted edge nodes, a direct global learning collaboration will be conducted to exchange newly learning information so that a group of distributed detection systems can collaborate with each other for an enhanced intrusion detection. Note that the discussed network channels in the edge enabled infrastructure will serve as a dedicated line for secure communications.

The entire model updating will be carried out in a periodic way. These two aspects will assure to generate up-to-date learning models for the robustness of intrusion detection.

4.2.4 Predictive Analytics

In this task, predictive analytics aims to offer a list of visualization tools for better perceiving cyber intrusions. Basic representation such as the confusion matrix can be provided to understand the detection accuracy. Given the values in a confusion matrix, important evaluation metrics such as sensitivity, specificity, precision, recall, F1-score, receiver operating characteristic (ROC) curve, and precision-recall (PR) curve can be calculated to further reflect the effectiveness of detection. Time series plot is also a great tool to visualize the time, duration, throughput, and other main factors of a malicious attack.

4.3 Threat Intelligence

Threat intelligence lies in the upper layer. As an important characteristic of "Software as a Service (SaaS)" from cloud computing technology, threat intelligence integrates a delivery model of many applications for intrusion detection, including a real-time traffic monitoring system and an emergency alarming system. The key of threat intelligence is threefold. First, an efficient and effective detection should be guaranteed at an edge node. Second, a proactive threat intelligence should keep monitoring the incoming traffic and learn the main causes of attacks from the traffic. Lastly, a robust and reliable response scheme should be enforced all the time, and continuous recovery mechanisms should be deployed as soon as possible.

4.4 Preliminary Study

4.4.1 Dataset

Two popular intrusion detection datasets are chosen from KDD'99 (Dheeru and Taniskidou, 2017) and UNSW-NB15 (Moustafa and Slay, 2016) for the evaluation. KDD'99 is originally developed by MIT Lincoln Labs, and the data were acquired by four gigabytes of compressed binary TCP dump data of a simulated military network environment in seven weeks. UNSW-NB15 was created in the Cyber Range Lab of the Australian Centre for Cyber Security, and the data are generated by capturing 100 GB of TCP dump data in a hybrid of the realistic modern normal activities and the synthetic contemporary attack behaviors from network traffic.

The dimensions of two datasets are 494 021 records by 42 features and 175 341 records by 45 features, respectively. In these two datasets, certain outliers are removed. PCA is performed as a feature selection method to create multiple subsets out of those two sets. The amount of information preserved from the original data is represented by Cumulative Proportion of Variance Explained (PVE), as presented in the right *Y*-axis of Figure 4.3.

4.4.2 Environmental Setup

The experiment is conducted by applying LR, RF, and C5.0, a DT-based model. Ensemble learning models are also developed by utilizing those three models. The experiment is using R language. It uses a computer with a CPU capability of 6 Intel Xeon X5660 CPUs × 2.8 GHz and a RAM of 23.987 GB.

Computational efficiency is evaluated first. In this step, a 5-fold cross-validation is performed on both datasets to obtain the prediction results. Confusion matrices are then formed given the values of prediction results. Based on the values, the mean error rate (MER) is calculated. In this

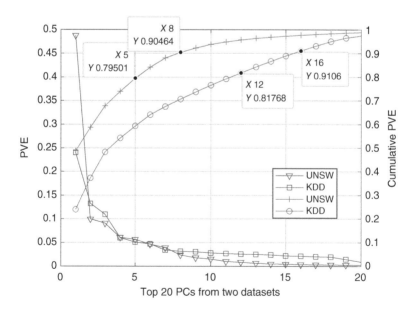

Figure 4.3 Feature selection on two datasets.

evaluation, 12 virtual machines are created to run the experiment. All machines run in parallel and start at the same time, the weight assignment scheme. To ensure the robustness of the prediction results, a 5-fold cross-validation is performed. Considering a diverse and heterogeneous networking environment, edge node 1 is evaluated with KDD data, while edge node 2 is evaluated with UNSW data. Multiple individual learning models and an ensemble learning model are all performed on the participating data. In this evaluation, the goal is to select the best-fitted local learning model, by deploying both datasets.

4.4.3 Performance Evaluation

The performance results are presented in Figure 4.3 and Tables 4.1–4.3. Note that the MER values presented in Tables 4.1–4.3 are truncated to four decimal places.

4.4.3.1 Computational Efficiency

After performing PCA, subsets from both datasets are created by separating the original data, 90% information-preserved data, and 80% information-preserved data. Figure 4.3 shows the top 20 principal components (PCs) that have retained the majority information of the original data. Four points are highlighted, indicating the number of PCs selected that are most close to the percentage of information to preserve. These highlighted four points also match the values presented in Tables 4.1 and 4.2.

Table 4.1 Result from KDD'99 data.

		KDD data (subset 1) (pre-processed: 36 features)	KDD data (subset 2) (pre-processed: 16 features)	KDD data (subset 3) (pre-processed: 12 features)
Dimension	Rows	481 676	481 676	481 676
	Columns	36	16	12
	PVE (%)	100	91.060	81.768
	Reduced	(12 345, 5)	(12 345, 26)	(12 345, 30)
MER	LR	0.0011	0.0014	0.0043
	C5.0	0.0010	0.0005	0.0010
Computing cost (s)	LR	145.47	59.87	64.90
	C5.0	440.38	198.80	147.88

Table 4.2 Results from UNSW-NB15 data.

		UNSW data (subset 4) (pre-processed: 40 features)	UNSW data (subset 5) (pre-processed: 8 features)	UNSW data (subset 6) (pre-processed: 5 features)
Dimension	Rows	170 957	170 957	170 957
	Columns	40	8	5
	PVE (%)	100	90.464	79.501
	Reduced	(4384, 5)	(4384, 37)	(4384, 40)
MER	LR	0.0638	0.0987	0.1109
	C5.0	0.0547	0.0578	0.0592
Computing cost (s)	LR	75.18	6.79	5.82
	C5.0	261.49	55.84	42.95

From the results, each subset retains the majority information of the original data, while huge storage spaces have been saved with 26 columns of subset 2, 30 columns of subset 3, 37 columns of subset 5, and 40 columns of subset 6. Assuming that each column possesses the same amount of storing units, the computational efficiency has greatly improved for the newly generated subsets. Meanwhile, the prediction performance from each virtual machine also reflects low learning errors, representing the robustness of prediction. Computational cost is also presented. Because of the nature of each machine learning model, the computational cost will vary.

4.4.3.2 Prediction Accuracy

In Table. 4.3, the predication accuracy is evaluated in terms of selecting the best-fitted local learning model. Multiple individual machine learning models and an ensemble learning model are involved. For edge node 1 filled with KDD data, 70% of the DT model and 30% of the LR model are involved to generate an ensemble learning model by following the optimal weight assignment scheme. Based on the performance presented in MER, the LR model has the lowest learning error, and it is selected as the local learning model for edge node 1.

For edge node 2 filled with UNSW data, 20% of the DT model, 10% LR model, and 70% of RF model are involved to generate an ensemble learning model. Based on the performance presented in MER, the RF model has the lowest learning error, and it is selected as the local learning model for edge node 2.

Table 4.3 Selection on the best-fitted local learning model.

Network	Data	Evaluation	Model 1 (DT)	Model 2 (LR)	Model 3 (RF)	Ensemble model
Edge node 1	KDD	Optimal weight (%)	70	30	—	—
		MER	**0.0006**	0.0052		0.0006
		Computing cost	186.18	181.10		357.80
Edge node 2	UNSW	Optimal weight (%)	20	10	70	—
		MER	0.0484	0.0728	**0.0426**	0.0430
		Computing cost	101.47	38.46	1948.10	2091.31

Usually, an ensemble learning model requires the integration of every involved individual learning model. Therefore, the computational overhead will last longer than the individual learning model. It is not necessary to always select the model with the lowest learning error. If the learning errors are similar in scale and all are in a desired data range, any of them could be adopted as the best-fitted ones. The objective is to ignore those models that provide unacceptable performance results.

4.5 Summary

In this chapter, three key modules of edge intelligence for intrusion detection are presented. The entire architecture includes edge cyberinfrastructure, edge AI engine, and threat intelligence. The proposed edge intelligence for intrusion detection is evaluated in terms of detection accuracy and computational efficiency. The preliminary results demonstrate its feasibility.

References

Theodora S Brisimi, Ruidi Chen, Theofanie Mela, Alex Olshevsky, Ioannis Ch Paschalidis, and Wei Shi. Federated learning of predictive models from federated electronic health records. *International Journal of Medical Informatics*, 112:59–67, 2018.

Dua Dheeru and Efi Karra Taniskidou. UCI machine learning repository, 2017. URL http://archive.ics.uci.edu/ml.

Nour Moustafa and Jill Slay. The evaluation of network anomaly detection systems: Statistical analysis of the UNSW-NB15 data set and the comparison with the KDD99 data set. *Information Security Journal: A Global Perspective*, 25(1–3):18–31, 2016.

Virginia Smith, Chao-Kai Chiang, Maziar Sanjabi, and Ameet S Talwalkar. Federated multi-task learning. In *Advances in Neural Information Processing Systems*, pages 4424–4434, 2017.

Shengjie Xu, Yi Qian, and Rose Qingyang Hu. Data-driven network intelligence for anomaly detection. *IEEE Network*, 33(3):88–95, 2019.

5

Robust Intrusion Detection

In this chapter, the research (Xu et al., 2019b) on robust intrusion detection is presented. First, the preliminaries of robust statistics are introduced. Then, the proposed robust intrusion detection is illustrated in terms of data pre-processing, individual learning, ensemble learning, and optimal sampling ratio selection. Lastly, the proposed study is empirically evaluated at each step in terms of balanced accuracy (BA).

5.1 Preliminaries

The use of robust statistics deals with identifying the presence of outliers. This section describes two approaches of robust statistics, namely, median absolute deviation (MAD) and Mahalanobis distance (MD).

5.1.1 Median Absolute Deviation

MAD is considered as a robust alternative to the standard deviation (Filzmoser et al., 2008; Pascoal et al., 2012). It is proposed to study the data with univariate information. The MAD of data is defined by

$$\text{MAD}(X) = c \cdot \text{med}_i(|x_i - \text{med}(X)|), \tag{5.1}$$

where med() denotes the median function and constant value $c = 1.4826$. MAD holds some advantages in computing, including computational efficiency.

5.1.2 Mahalanobis Distance

The generalized Euclidean distance can be utilized to study outlier detection in data with multivariate information. MD is one of the forms from the

Cybersecurity in Intelligent Networking Systems, First Edition.
Shengjie Xu, Yi Qian, and Rose Qingyang Hu.
© 2023 John Wiley & Sons Ltd. Published 2023 by John Wiley & Sons Ltd.

generalized Euclidean distance. In particular, given a data point $x_i \in \mathbb{R}^p$ with multivariate information, the square of the generalized Euclidean distance is defined as

$$D_M^2(x_i) = (x_i - \mu)^T \Sigma^{-1}(x_i - \mu), \tag{5.2}$$

where μ is the mean vector of the data X and Σ^{-1} is a robust estimate of the covariance matrix.

For normally distributed data that is under a feature space of $\mathbb{R}^p$, the squared MD follows approximately χ_p^2, namely, a Chi-squared distribution with p degrees of freedom (Johnson et al., 2002). For detecting apparent anomalies in a data with multivariate information, the challenge of applying distance-based approaches is that a value of threshold should be numerically determined for an observation being an outlier. As described in Pascoal et al. (2012), the authors stated that an outlier threshold for the MD would be defined as the square root of the 0.975 quantile in a data with χ_2^2 distribution.

5.2 Robust Intrusion Detection

In this section, the problem statement is firstly formulated, followed by each step of the proposed robust intrusion detection. The current challenges to train a robust intrusion detection classifier are the difficulty to acquire fully labeled traffic data and accuracy problems of one single classifier. The proposed scheme is illustrated in four steps, as shown in Figure 5.1.

5.2.1 Problem Formulation

Let $\mathcal{X}$ denote the feature spaces of network traffic and $\mathcal{Y} = \{+1, -1\}$ the labeling classes in the response variable, where +1 stands for a specific type of malicious intrusion and −1 stands for a normal traffic. In large collected traffic data $\{(x_i, y_i) \in \mathcal{X} \times \mathcal{Y}\}$, the first objective is to identify two separate

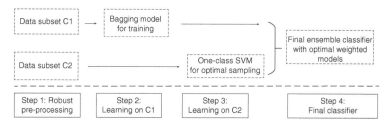

Figure 5.1 The proposed robust intrusion detection.

data subsets where one contains robustly pre-processed anomalies and the other contains the remaining unlabeled data.

The second objective is to build a learning model $f : \mathcal{X} \to \mathcal{Y}$ in a robust way so that the anomalies inside of the upcoming network traffic could be effectively recognized and distinguished.

5.2.2 Step 1: Robust Data Pre-processing

The objective of this process is to explore the properties of traffic features to identify the apparent anomalies. From this perspective, this step will not only record those anomalies for further weighted training purposes but also lead to significant computational advantages for large-scale data.

First, log transformation is applied on the original numerical data. The base 10 logarithm is utilized to convert the data. This step can shape highly skewed distributions to be less skewed, and it will be a boost for the robust scaling. Additionally, it is also crucial to transform the patterns of the data more interpretable (Lane et al., 2008).

Second, the distribution of the collected data should be identified (Xu et al., 2017). If the collected data follow or approximately follow the normal distribution, then the median and MAD from robust statistics will be considered to scale the data. If not, then a robust estimator S_n is considered to scale the collected data. S_n was proposed by the authors in Rousseeuw and Croux (1993) to be an alternative to MAD, and it is denoted as $S_n = c \cdot \mathrm{med}_i \{ \mathrm{med}_i |x_i - x_j| \}$. S_n holds a Gaussian efficiency of 58%, whereas MAD holds 37%. S_n is proven to perform well on both the normal data and the non-normal data.

The scaling process by the coordinate-wise median and robust estimator will be applied on the log-transformed data. There are two options. If the log-transformed data possesses normal distribution, then the data are scaled by $\frac{X - \mathrm{med}_i(x)}{\mathrm{MAD}(X)}$. If the newly log-transformed data possess non-normal distribution, then the data are scaled by $\frac{X - \mathrm{med}_i(x)}{S_n(X)}$. Following this approach, the mean is replaced by the median, and the empirical standard deviation by MAD and S_n, respectively. This step transforms the collected data to new and robust data.

Given the previous steps, the last step is operated by computing the squared MD of data. The 0.975 quantile in a χ_k^2 distribution is considered as a separation boundary for anomalies. The identified ones will be recorded and regarded as the data subset of robustly pre-processed anomalies and will then be further trained along with the normal traffic. The remaining data will be recorded and considered as the data subset of filtered network traffic and will then be further trained. These steps form the general idea to detect apparent anomalies, especially when majority types of anomalies appeared.

5.2.3 Step 2: Bagging for Labeled Anomalies

As the robustly pre-processed anomalies are recorded, this data subset is treated as data with a relatively robust labeling class that corresponds to specific network anomalies. In this step, the data subset is newly formed by concatenating the anomalies and the normal traffic and then further trained by an effective supervised learning model.

There are many options in machine learning models. As a popular supervised learning model, decision tree is usually considered as a supervised learning model to discover network anomalies (Buczak and Guven, 2016). However, regular decision tree models typically suffer from high variance (James et al., 2013), and they will bring a high amount of change if a trained learning model f is estimated on a different training dataset. Given the fact that the data subset of robustly preprocessed anomalies is not a large portion of the collected traffic, it is even critical to apply a supervised learning model that is not prone to obtaining a high-variance result. In this step, bagging (bootstrap aggregation) is adopted to train on the robustly pre-processed anomalies, in which it can offer the ability to reduce the variance of a learning model and further avoid overfitting.

The bagging method relies on multiple base learning models and a statistical resampling approach of bootstrap. By utilizing bootstrap, repeated samples are taken from the data subset of robustly pre-processed anomalies C_1. In this approach, T different bootstrapped training datasets are generated, and each separate learning model $f_{C_1}^i(x)$ is built upon each training set, respectively. The resulting predictions $\hat{y}_{C_1}^i$ are represented in a qualitative way, and they are processed based on a majority vote from the class predicted by each of the T base learning models. The details of learning on the data subset of robustly pre-processed anomalies are presented in Algorithm 5.1.

5.2.4 Step 3: One-class SVM for Unlabeled Samples

The traditional supervised learning techniques may not be directly applied in this step, as the labeling class in this data subset remains in an inaccessible and unreliable state. Additionally, as presented in Zhang et al. (2017) and Zhang et al. (2018) previously, a semi-supervised learning model would naturally provide a better use of the remaining anomalies and provide better performance along with the unlabeled network traffic. In this step, one-class

---

Algorithm 5.1 Step 2 in data subset C_1

1: Inputs: the data subset of robustly pre-processed anomalies C_1, an integer T;

2: From $i = 1$ to T:

    1. Obtain bootstrap sample S_i from C_1,

    2. Construct learning model $f^i_{C_1}(x)$,

3: Output: the learning model $f^*_{C_1}$, obtained by conducting a majority vote from $\{f^1_{C_1}, \ldots, f^i_{C_1}, \ldots, f^T_{C_1}\}$.

---

classification is performed, and then an algorithm is proposed to obtain an optimal sampling ratio on the one-class data so that the BA of the learning model is more robust.

5.2.4.1 One-class Classification

This problem is formulated as the one-class classification problem. One-class classification can be performed under three general cases: positive subsets only; positive subsets and some amount of poorly sampled negative subsets; and positive and unlabeled data. In this study, One-Class Support Vector Machine (OCSVM) is considered to perform on the positive and unlabeled data.

Assuming $\mathbf{x}$ is the training set as input, the kernel mapping function $\phi(\cdot)$ maps an input to the feature space F. In other words, the goal of a Gaussian kernel is to solve the separation problem by searching for a hyperplane that separates a desired fraction of the training subsets from the origin of the feature space F. The kernel mapping function $\phi(\cdot)$ helps to find the hyperplane from the original feature space F to a kernel space F'. In this case, radial basis function $K(x_i, x'_i) = \exp(-\gamma \sum_{j=1}^{p} (x_{ij} - x_{i'j})^2)$ (James et al., 2013) is chosen as the kernel for training and predicting. The main objective can be formulated as follows:

$$\min_{\mathbf{w}, \xi, \rho} \frac{1}{2}\|\mathbf{w}\|^2 + \frac{1}{vl}\sum_{i=1}^{l}\xi_i - \rho \tag{5.3}$$

$$\text{s.t. } (\mathbf{w} \cdot \phi(\mathbf{x}_i)) \geq \rho - \xi_i, \quad i = 1, 2, \ldots, l, \xi_i \geq 0,$$

where l is the size of the training set and ξ_i is a vector of slack variables for data observation i, which determines the rejected patterns based on the hyperplane. v is a regularization parameter, formally defined as "an upper bound on the fraction of training errors and a lower bound of the fraction of support vectors" (Amer et al., 2013). Based on the Lagrangian method discussed in Xiao et al. (2015), the dual problem of OCSVM can be transformed to

$$\max_{\alpha} \ -\frac{\alpha^T Q \alpha}{2}$$

$$\text{s.t. } 0 \leq \alpha_i \leq \frac{1}{vl}, \quad \sum_{i=1}^{l} \alpha_i = 1, \tag{5.4}$$

where Q is the kernel matrix and α is the Lagrange multipliers.

5.2.4.2 Algorithm of Optimal Sampling Ratio Section

To achieve a high BA from a robustly trained learning model, the optimal sampling ratio is important to determine on the one-class data. In the second step, an optimal sampling ratio selection scheme is proposed on the one-class data. A vector **s** of sampling ratios is provided to select the optimal learning model. Given the data subset of filtered network traffic C_2, the data observations with a positive class are firstly extracted by selecting the sampling ratio from vector **s** with l elements (e.g. $\mathbf{s} = \{s_1, \ldots, s_j, \ldots, s_l\}$). A floor function is applied to acquire the size of a sampled subset created from the origin observations with positive class. The selected sample subset is then regarded as a training subset with positive class. In the next step, the process of model training and validation is conducted in several training subsets created by the vector **s**. Note that during the training process, kernel function, data normalization, and regularization parameter setting should also be determined.

After processing the aforementioned steps, the remaining subset with positive class is combined with the data without label to form a test subset with both positive and negative classes. The candidate learning models are derived from several test subsets created by different sampling ratios, and the optimal learning model is finally evaluated in this stage. The main procedures of this step are illustrated in Algorithm 5.2 and (Xu et al., 2019a).

Algorithm 5.2 can be applied to a sample subset for learning purposes. In this part, multiple subsets are created from the original data, and they are sampled differently for training multiple models. As the goal is to select the best model with the best optimal sampling ratio among those subsets, it would be an impractical idea to train all the models in a serial way, as it will cause too much latency. As discussed previously, achieving a low latency is critical for intrusion detection on the edge. Thus, a parallel processing way of model learning will be offered by the support of edge computing. In this work, multiple virtual machines are created, and they are launched to accommodate multiple subsets and then to adjust to the different sampling ratios. Let $V_{a,u,v}$ be the index vector of virtual machines created in an

---

Algorithm 5.2 The selection of optimal sampling ratio

1: Inputs: data with positive class D_p and data without label D_u from the data subset of filtered network traffic C_2;

2: Initialize training set S_{ta}, test set S_{te}, vector of candidate sampling ratio **s**;

3: Form the training set S_{ta} by selecting $\mathbf{s}_i$ from D_p;

4: Form the test set S_{te} by combining $D_p \setminus S_{ta}$ and D_u;

5: Train an OCSVM model f_j by only the features of S_{ta} (meanwhile keeping response variable as 'NULL');

    1. Apply radial basis function as kernel,

    2. Normalize the entire data,

    3. Set the regularization parameter v,

6: Perform k-fold cross-validation;

7: Apply the OCSVM model to S_{te};

8: Outputs: the optimal learning model $f_{C_2}^*$ and the optimal sampling ratio $\mathbf{s}_i^*$.

---

edge computing node and $f_{a,u,v}$ be the learning model trained at the corresponding machine, where a represents the index of a specific intrusion, u represents the index of subset, and v represents the index of sampling ratio. Based on the evaluation metrics (e.g. recall, precision, and BA), an optimal learning model f^* and sampling ratio $\mathbf{s}_i^*$ can be chosen.

5.2.5 Step 4: The Final Classifier

In this step, a scheme is proposed to form a weighted ensemble model and further determine the final optimal learning model. This proposed scheme is inspired by ensemble learning. In machine learning, the ensemble learning approach is widely utilized for data learning tasks. Ensemble learning adopts multiple individual learning models together to obtain a better predictive performance than these models alone. In some cases, the performance of ensemble learning beats an individual learning model. In this step, an ensemble model is considered as an enhanced learning model, which is based on a linear combination of the two individual models trained in the data subsets of robustly pre-processed anomalies and the filtered network traffic, respectively. On forming this ensemble model, a weight vector $\mathbf{w}_{ensemble} = \{w_{model1}, w_{model2}\}$ with numerical entries in $\{0.1, 0.2, \ldots, 0.9\}$ is initialized. In this linear combination, each individual model is assigned with a weight, and the sum of all weights is 100%. The previously trained models in each data subset will be treated as individual models, and they will be applied onto the entire data subset to generate the ensemble model. The criterion of selecting the final optimal learning model is based on the corresponding evaluation metric that significantly reflects the effectiveness and robustness of the training model.

In an edge computing node, a virtual machine will be assigned to enumerate all the possible combinations and then further select the final ensemble learning model given the combination of individual models, which provides a satisfied criterion (e.g. mean error rate). Meanwhile, the weight vector of each model will be recorded. After finalizing the weight vector, the edge node will compare the final ensemble learning model with the involved two independent individual models and then select the final optimal learning model.

Algorithm 5.3 Optimal weighted ensemble learning

1: Inputs: The data subset of robustly preprocessed anomalies C_1 and the individual model $f^*_{C_1}$ optimally trained in it, the data subset of filtered network traffic C_2 and the individual model $f^*_{C_2}$ optimally trained in it, the entire data subset C_{total}, and an initialized weight vector $\mathbf{w}_{ensemble}$;

2: Generate a list of weight combinations which the summation of all elements equal to 1.0;

3: Apply $f^*_{C_1}$ and $f^*_{C_2}$ onto the entire data subset C_{total} and record the mean error rate respectively;

4: Train an ensemble learning model on the C_{total}

    1. For each weight combination, obtain the result from ensemble model,

    2. Obtain the index of the weight combination with the minimum mean error rate

    3. Record the ensemble learning model $f^*_{C_{total}}$

5: Compare the individual learning models and ensemble model using validation approach

6: Output: the final optimal learning model, namely $\hat{f}^*_{C_{total}}$

The obtained ensemble learning model will most likely be the most suitable model, as indicated by Buczak and Guven (2016) and James et al. (2013). However, it is possible that the ensemble model may not eventually be chosen as the final optimal learning model. It is not necessary to always select the model with lowest learning error or BA. If the learning errors (e.g. values of BA, recall, and precision) are similar in scale and not deviated in large scale, and all are in a desired data range, any of them could be adopted as the best-fitted ones. The objective is to ignore those models that provide unacceptable performance results. The main procedures of this step are illustrated in Algorithm 5.3.

5.3 Experimental and Evaluation

In this section, the experimental setup and the details of performance evaluations are presented.

5.3.1 Experiment Setup

5.3.1.1 Datasets

Two popular intrusion detection datasets are used for this performance study. The first utilized dataset for evaluation is from the KDD'99 (Dheeru and Taniskidou, 2017). It was originally developed by MIT Lincoln Labs, and the data were acquired by four gigabytes of compressed binary TCP dump data of a simulated military network environment in seven weeks. The original dimension of the entire data is 494 021 records by 42 features. In this first experiment, the performance evaluation of individual network intrusion is targeted. Specifically, two Probe attacks, namely, *Port sweep* and *SATAN*, and two flooding attacks, namely, *Back* and *Neptune*, are investigated. *Port sweep*, *SATAN*, *Back*, *Neptune*, and normal traffic contain 1040, 1589, 2203, 107 201, and 97 278 number of observations, respectively. The second utilized dataset for evaluation is from UNSW-NB15 (Moustafa and Slay, 2015, 2016). UNSW-NB15 was created in the Cyber Range Lab of the Australian Centre for Cyber Security, and the data were generated by capturing 100 GB of TCP dump data in a hybrid of the realistic modern normal activities and the synthetic contemporary attack behaviors in network traffic. The original dimension of the entire data is 175 341 records by 45 features. In this second experiment, the performance evaluation of individual network intrusion is also targeted. Similar to the first dataset, two corresponding Probe attacks, namely, *Analysis* and *Exploits*, and two corresponding flooding attacks, namely, *Backdoor* and *DoS* are also investigated in the UNSW-NB15 dataset. *Analysis*, *Exploits*, *Backdoor*, *DoS*, and normal traffic contain 2000, 33 393, 1746, 12 264, and 56 000 number of observations, respectively.

For feature engineering of these two datasets, some of the features are removed, as explained in Xu et al. (2017). For individual attack of both datasets, the corresponding data observations are extracted and combined with normal traffic data. The sample ratio is considered in the range of 0.6 and 0.8.

5.3.1.2   Environmental Setup

The experiment is conducted by following the four steps of the proposed data-driven robust network intrusion detection scheme. The experiment uses a workstation for edge computing with a CPU capability of 6 Intel Xeon X5660 CPUs × 2.8 GHz and a RAM of 23.987 GB. Confusion matrices are presented, and important evaluation metrics are then formed given the values of prediction results.

5.3.1.3   Evaluation Metrics

The basic evaluation metrics such as true positive (TP), true negative (TN), false positive (FP), and false negative (FN) can be calculated from the confusion matrix. Advanced evaluation metrics such as accuracy (ACC), sensitivity (i.e. Recall), specificity, positive predictive value (PPV) (i.e. precision), negative predictive value (NPV), and BA are all considered in this work. The equations of those metrics are defined as follows:

- Accuracy = (TP + TN)/(TP+TN+FP+FN),
- Sensitivity (i.e. Recall) = TP/(TP+FN),
- Specificity = TN/(TN+FP),
- Positive predictive value / Precision = TP/(TP+FP),
- Negative predictive value = TN/(TN+FN),
- Balanced accuracy = (specificity + sensitivity)/2.

5.3.2   Performance Evaluation

5.3.2.1   Step 1

In Table 5.1, the results from the robustly pre-processed data subset in step 1 are shown. By applying robust scaling and setting out a threshold for Chi-square distribution, the apparent anomalies are identified and grouped

Table 5.1   Performance evaluation on step 1.

		Probe attack		Flooding attack	
		Port sweep	*SATAN*	*Back*	*Neptune*
KDD	Original	1040	1589	2203	107 201
	C_2	116	50	1208	107 032
		Analysis	*Exploits*	*Backdoor*	*DoS*
UNSW-NB15	Original	2000	33 393	1746	12 264
	C_2	1967	32 776	1729	12 036

Table 5.2 Performance evaluation of probe and flooding attacks in KDD data (step 2).

Predicted		Reference		
	Port sweep	FALSE	TRUE	Balanced accuracy
	FALSE	2800	4	0.9947
	TRUE	4	441	
	SATAN	FALSE	TRUE	Balanced accuracy
	FALSE	2791	2	0.9957
	TRUE	6	758	
	Back	FALSE	TRUE	Balanced accuracy
	FALSE	2810	0	0.9989
	TRUE	1	474	
	Neptune	FALSE	TRUE	Balanced accuracy
	FALSE	2782	3	0.9879
	TRUE	2	85	

in data subset C_1. The filtered network traffic is preserved as a data subset C_2 and further studied in the remaining steps.

5.3.2.2 Step 2
In Tables 5.2 and 5.3, the results of the confusion matrix from robustly pre-processed data subset C_1 are shown. From the results, there is barely any type I error (i.e. FP) in all investigated network anomalies. In other words, prediction error on the normal traffic remains very low. Type II error (i.e. FN) occurs when testing is performed. However, considering the BA from all eight network anomalies is satisfied, the performance results could be continuously improved, as more network traffic data is collected. Besides those errors, the rates of TP and TN remain high.

5.3.2.3 Step 3
The performance evaluation results are presented in Tables 5.4–5.7, and Figures 5.2–5.5. Note that the results presented in Tables 5.4–5.7 are truncated to four decimal places.

By applying Algorithm 5.2 to the training and predicting, the results are obtained and presented in Tables 5.4–5.7. For the general probe and flooding attack, eight network anomalies are investigated. The vector **s** of the candidate sampling ratio is created as **s** = {0.6, 0.7, 0.8}. A seed valued "2018" is chosen as a generator for the sampling so that the reproduction of the

Table 5.3 Performance evaluation of probe and flooding attacks in UNSW-NB15 data (step 2).

Predicted		Reference		
	Analysis	FALSE	TRUE	Balanced accuracy
	FALSE	1308	2	0.8429
	TRUE	5	11	
	Exploits	FALSE	TRUE	Balanced accuracy
	FALSE	1303	14	0.9714
	TRUE	14	287	
	Backdoor	FALSE	TRUE	Balanced accuracy
	FALSE	1310	0	0.8125
	TRUE	3	5	
	DoS	FALSE	TRUE	Balanced accuracy
	FALSE	1294	5	0.9580
	TRUE	10	115	

Table 5.4 Performance evaluation on probe attack in KDD data (step 3).

Attack			Probe attack			
Attack category		*Port Sweep*			*SATAN*	
Proportions of network anomalies in C_2		116/91 819			50/91 753	
Sampling ratio	0.6	0.7	0.8	0.6	0.7	0.8
Accuracy	0.9999	0.9998	1.0000	0.9873	0.9893	0.9923
Recall	0.8863	0.5937	**1.0000**	0.7777	**0.833 33**	0.7500
Specificity	0.9999	0.9999	0.9999	0.9873	0.9893	0.9923
Precision	0.9750	0.9500	0.9523	0.0119	0.0101	0.8451
NPV	0.9999	0.9998	1.0000	0.9999	0.9999	1.0000
Balanced accuracy	0.9431	0.7968	**0.9999**	0.8825	**0.9113**	0.8712

experiment can be verified in the next attempts. The proportions of network anomalies shown in the third column is based on the number of anomalies over the total number of anomalies and normal traffic. In this table, 24 virtual machines are running in a parallel way so that one machine can instantly launch an effective model and update the model efficiently.

Table 5.5 Performance evaluation on flooding attack in KDD data (step 3).

Attack	Flooding attack					
Attack category	*Back*			*Neptune*		
Proportions of network anomalies in C_2	1208/92 911			107 032/198 735		
Sampling ratio	0.6	0.7	0.8	0.6	0.7	0.8
Accuracy	0.9996	0.9997	0.9997	0.9686	0.9735	0.9812
Recall	**0.9250**	0.9194	0.9041	**0.9015**	0.8978	0.9008
Specificity	1.0000	1.0000	1.0000	1.0000	1.0000	1.0000
Precision	1.0000	1.0000	1.0000	1.0000	1.0000	1.0000
NPV	0.9996	0.9996	0.9997	0.9560	0.9654	0.9774
Balanced accuracy	**0.9625**	0.9597	0.9520	**0.9507**	0.9489	0.9504

Table 5.6 Performance evaluation on probe attack in UNSW-NB15 data (step 3).

Attack	Probe attack					
Attack category	*Analysis*			*Exploits*		
Proportions of network anomalies in C_2	1967/55 347			32 776/86 156		
Sampling ratio	0.6	0.7	0.8	0.6	0.7	0.8
Accuracy	0.9927	0.9949	0.9967	0.8573	0.8931	0.9221
Recall	0.4961	0.5340	**0.5484**	0.2761	**0.3127**	0.2880
Specificity	1.0000	0.9999	1.0000	0.9999	0.9999	0.9999
Precision	1.0000	0.9968	0.9953	0.9994	0.9993	0.9973
NPV	0.9926	0.9948	0.9966	0.8490	0.8876	0.9196
Balanced accuracy	0.7480	0.7669	**0.7742**	0.6380	**0.6563**	0.6439

After performing 3-fold cross-validation on the training set, multiple learning models are obtained, and then, the models are applied to each newly combined test set. Evaluation metrics are reflected from different sampling ratios. The best results of each specific intrusion are highlighted in bold font, in terms of recall and BA. Tables 5.4–5.7 show that the precision of the learned model is 100% (except for the *SATAN* attack as the majority of this intrusion is already identified by step 1, causing a

Table 5.7 Performance evaluation on flooding attack in UNSW-NB15 data (step 3).

Attack	Flooding attack					
Attack category		*Backdoor*			*DoS*	
Proportions of network anomalies in C_2		1729/55 109			12 036/65 416	
Sampling ratio	0.6	0.7	0.8	0.6	0.7	0.8
Accuracy	0.9928	0.9948	0.9964	0.9616	0.9734	0.9808
Recall	0.4383	**0.4612**	0.4418	0.5367	**0.5812**	0.5596
Specificity	0.9999	0.9999	0.9999	0.9999	0.9998	0.9999
Precision	0.9934	0.9958	0.9870	0.9988	0.9971	0.9962
NPV	0.9928	0.9948	0.9964	0.9599	0.9724	0.9804
Balanced accuracy	0.7191	**0.7306**	0.7209	0.7683	**0.7905**	0.7784

low number of training size in step 3 and its precision value). This metric explains the wellness of the model in identifying only anomalies, and it also speaks for the percentage of real anomalies in a subset. The metric recall measures the wellness of the model in identifying all anomalies, and it shows the capability of a model detecting an anomalous behavior when it occurred. The highest value in recall corresponds to the highest value in BA, respectively. From the overall results, the balanced detection accuracy of each intrusion is satisfied.

Figures 5.2–5.5 present the receiver operating characteristic (ROC) curve and the precision-recall (PR) curve from the attacks. A ROC curve represents the type I and type II errors for all possible thresholds simultaneously, with x-axis being the FP rate and y-axis being the TP rate. Figures 5.4 and 5.5 display the ROC curve for the optimal semi-supervised learning model on the test data. The area under the ROC curve, namely, area under the curve (AUC), is used to evaluate the overall performance of a learning model by summarizing over all possible thresholds. A practical and ideal ROC curve will hug the upper-left-hand corner; therefore, the larger the AUC, the better performance the learning model can provide (James et al., 2013). From the calculation, the ROC AUC values for eight network anomalies are 0.9999, 0.9947, 0.9999, and 0.9999 for the KDD dataset and 0.9186, 0.7314, 0.8622, and 0.9002 for the UNSW-NB15 dataset, which are all close to the maximum of 1. Note that the AUC values for three anomalies are the same, therefore the ROC curves of these three in Figure 5.4 are overlapped.

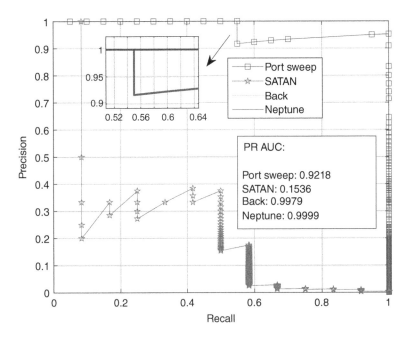

Figure 5.2 PR curve - KDD.

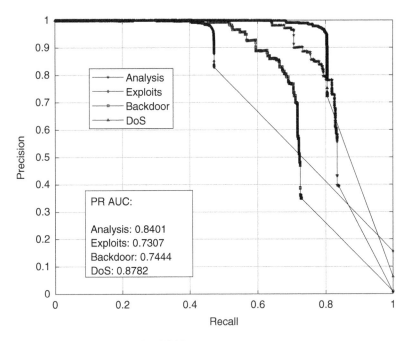

Figure 5.3 PR curve - UNSW-NB15.

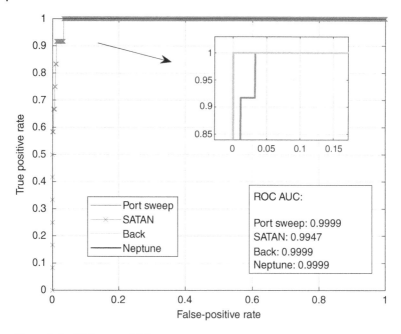

Figure 5.4   ROC curve - KDD.

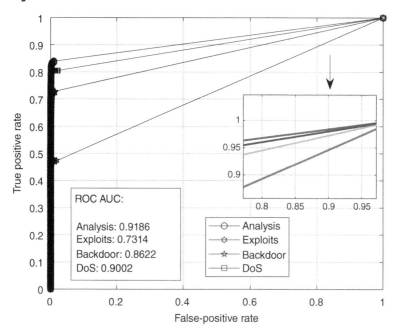

Figure 5.5   ROC curve - UNSW-NB15.

Figures 5.2 and 5.3 display the PR curve for the optimal semi-supervised learning model on the test set. A PR curve reflects the relationship between recall and precision. It is considered to be more informative when there is a high class imbalance in the data (Davis and Goadrich, 2006), as found in Tables 5.1, 5.6, and 5.7. The PR curve is preferable when highly imbalanced and positive samples are much less. In Davis and Goadrich (2006), the authors stated that a practical and ideal PR curve is to hug the upper-right-hand corner. From the figure, the optimal learning models are very robust and effective under an imbalanced scenario with network traffic data composed of anomalies and normal data. By utilizing the trapezoidal rule for integral, the PR AUC values for eight network anomalies are 0.9218, 0.1536, 0.9979, and 0.9999 for the KDD dataset and 0.8401, 0.7307, 0.7444, and 0.8782 for the UNSW-NB15 dataset. Except for value from *SATAN* (as the majority of this intrusion is already identified by step 1, causing a low number of training size in step 3), whose number of observations only contain 50 in this case, the rest of the values are all close to the maximum of 1. Based on the performance results from both ROC and PR curves, the trained models are built considerably robustly.

5.3.2.4   Step 4

In Table 5.8, the predication accuracy is evaluated in terms of selecting the best-fitted local learning model. Two individual learning models and an ensemble learning model are involved. Based on the computational results of the minimum BA, 50% of bagging and 50% of one-class model are finally determined and then involved to generate an ensemble learning model by following the optimal weight assignment algorithm in Algorithm 5.3 on an edge node validating the KDD dataset. Based on the performance presented in BA, an ensemble model for *Neptune* and three f_1^* models for *Port sweep*, *SATAN*, and *Back* are selected as the optimal local learning model. For the validation work on the UNSW-NB15 data, all the four ensemble models are determined and then selected as the optimal local learning model for each intrusion.

Usually, an ensemble learning model requires the integration of all the involved individual models. Therefore, the computational overhead will last longer than the individual learning model. It is not necessary to always select the model with lowest learning error or BA. If the learning errors (e.g. values of BA, recall, and precision) are similar in scale and not deviated in a large scale, and all are in a desired data range, any of them could be adopted as the best-fitted ones. The objective is to ignore those models that provide unacceptable performance results.

Table 5.8 Performance comparison among two individual models and the ensemble model (step 4).

Dataset	Category	Model f_1^* (trained from step 2)	Model f_1^* (trained from step 3)	Ensemble model f_e^* (trained from step 4)
		Balanced accuracy		
Validation set of KDD	Port sweep	**0.9857**	0.6591	0.9848
	SATAN	**0.9924**	0.5337	0.9918
	Back	**0.9995**	0.8507	**0.9995**
	Neptune	0.9046	0.9496	**0.9869**
Validation set of UNSW-NB15	Analysis	0.5219	0.8097	**0.8317**
	Exploits	0.8423	0.7707	**0.9377**
	Backdoor	0.5021	0.7829	**0.7850**
	DoS	0.5336	0.8325	**0.8472**

5.4 Summary

In this chapter, a proposed scheme of robust intrusion detection is presented. First, the preliminaries of robust statistics are introduced. Then, the proposed robust intrusion detection is illustrated in terms of data pre-processing, individual learning, ensemble learning, and optimal sampling ratio selection. Lastly, the proposed study is empirically evaluated at each step in terms of BA.

References

Mennatallah Amer, Markus Goldstein, and Slim Abdennadher. Enhancing one-class support vector machines for unsupervised anomaly detection. In *Proceedings of the ACM SIGKDD Workshop on Outlier Detection and Description*, pages 8–15. ACM, 2013.

Anna L Buczak and Erhan Guven. A survey of data mining and machine learning methods for cyber security intrusion detection. *IEEE Communication Surveys and Tutorials*, 18(2):1153–1176, 2016.

Jesse Davis and Mark Goadrich. The relationship between precision-recall and ROC curves. In *Proceedings of the 23rd International Conference on Machine learning*, pages 233–240. ACM, 2006.

Dua Dheeru and Efi Karra Taniskidou. UCI machine learning repository, 2017. URL http://archive.ics.uci.edu/ml.

Peter Filzmoser, Ricardo Maronna, and Mark Werner. Outlier identification in high dimensions. *Computational Statistics and Data Analysis*, 52(3):1694–1711, 2008.

Gareth James, Daniela Witten, Trevor Hastie, and Robert Tibshirani. *An Introduction to Statistical Learning*, volume 112. Springer, 2013.

Richard Arnold Johnson, Dean W Wichern, et al. *Applied Multivariate Statistical Analysis*, volume 5. Prentice Hall, Upper Saddle River, NJ, 2002.

David M. Lane. Online Statistics Education: A Multimedia Course of Study. Rice University, 2008. http://onlinestatbook.com/

David Lane, Joan Lu, Camille Peres, Emily Zitek, et al. Online statistics: An interactive multimedia course of study. *Retrieved January*, 29:2009, 2008.

Nour Moustafa and Jill Slay. UNSW-NB15: A comprehensive data set for network intrusion detection systems (UNSW-NB15 network data set). In *Military Communications and Information Systems Conference (MilCIS), 2015*, pages 1–6. IEEE, 2015.

Nour Moustafa and Jill Slay. The evaluation of network anomaly detection systems: Statistical analysis of the UNSW-NB15 data set and the comparison with the KDD99 data set. *Information Security Journal: A Global Perspective*, 25(1–3):18–31, 2016.

Cláudia Pascoal, M Rosario De Oliveira, Rui Valadas, Peter Filzmoser, Paulo Salvador, and António Pacheco. Robust feature selection and robust PCA for internet traffic anomaly detection. In *INFOCOM, 2012 Proceedings IEEE*, pages 1755–1763. IEEE, 2012.

Peter J Rousseeuw and Christophe Croux. Alternatives to the median absolute deviation. *Journal of the American Statistical Association*, 88(424):1273–1283, 1993.

Yingchao Xiao, Huangang Wang, and Wenli Xu. Parameter selection of Gaussian Kernel for one-class SVM. *IEEE Transactions on Cybernetics*, 45(5):941–953, 2015.

Shengjie Xu, Yi Qian, and Rose Qingyang Hu. A data-driven preprocessing scheme on anomaly detection in big data applications. In *2017 IEEE Conference on Computer Communications Workshops (INFOCOM WKSHPS)*, pages 814–819. IEEE, 2017.

Shengjie Xu, Yi Qian, and Rose Qingyang Hu. A semi-supervised learning approach for network anomaly detection in fog computing. In *2019 IEEE International Conference on Communications (ICC)*, pages 1–6. IEEE, 2019a.

Shengjie Xu, Yi Qian, and Rose Qingyang Hu. Data-driven edge intelligence for robust network anomaly detection. *IEEE Transactions on Network Science and Engineering*, 7(3):1481–1492, 2019b.

Ya-Lin Zhang, Longfei Li, Jun Zhou, Xiaolong Li, Yujiang Liu, Yuanchao Zhang, and Zhi-Hua Zhou. POSTER: A PU learning based system for potential malicious URL detection. In *Proceedings of the 2017 ACM SIGSAC Conference on Computer and Communications Security*, pages 2599–2601. ACM, 2017.

Ya-Lin Zhang, Longfei Li, Jun Zhou, Xiaolong Li, and Zhi-Hua Zhou. Anomaly detection with partially observed anomalies. In *Companion of the The Web Conference 2018 on The Web Conference 2018*, pages 639–646. International World Wide Web Conferences Steering Committee, 2018.

6

Efficient Pre-processing Scheme for Anomaly Detection

In this chapter, the research (Xu et al., 2017) on an efficient pre-processing scheme for anomaly detection is presented. First, a few related studies and background of principal component analysis (PCA) are introduced. The proposed scheme is then presented. The goal of the efficient pre-processing scheme aims to achieve high detection accuracy and low computational overhead. Lastly, a case study is empirically conducted in terms of detection accuracy and dimensionality reduction.

6.1 Efficient Anomaly Detection

Efficient anomaly detection mechanisms are becoming an urgent and critical topic in the presence of big data applications. In this research, we propose a data-driven pre-processing scheme on anomaly detection that incorporates a dimension reduction algorithm and present a real-time learning idea for big data applications. Specifically, the extensive use of the robust data pre-processing and a real-time data learning approach are discussed. The proposed robust data pre-processing scheme not only preserves the critical property of dimension reduction for high-dimensional data but also introduces a robust detection boundary to the presence of outliers. Real-time learning is inspired by online learning, which differs from batch-based data processing that performs data learning on an entire batch of dataset. Real-time learning aims to make progress with each example it looks at. Detailed discussions are provided for the justification of this scheme. A case study is presented to demonstrate the feasibility of the proposed scheme.

Despite its eminent achievements, the growing popularity and development of big data applications are also bringing serious vulnerabilities and threats to the security and privacy of sensitive information (Xu et al., 2014, 2018, 2015, 2017b; Xu and Qian, 2015). Among the massive big data

Cybersecurity in Intelligent Networking Systems, First Edition.
Shengjie Xu, Yi Qian, and Rose Qingyang Hu.

applications that have been adopted and processed all over the world, threats based on anomalous behaviors against these applications have never been more outrageous. As online threats are evolving in the virtual environment, the well-known Denial of Service (DoS) attack is constantly disrupting online operations among big data applications. DoS is carried out by sorts of requests for a service and must be detected before it breaks down the system server. Because of those large numbers of simultaneous requests, this type of attacks usually causes anomalous behavior in the network traffic.

Intrusion detection systems (IDSs) are complicated computing system tools that monitor malicious behaviors or detect violations on a specific operation. An IDS usually relies on two main approaches to detect intrusions that differ in the way the data are analyzed and processed (Dalmazo et al., 2016). The first approach corresponds to a search for evidence of an attack based on signatures of other similar attacks, while the second approach consists of a search for deviations from the appropriate behavior found in periodic observations of the system (Stallings, 2006). The principal advantage of the signature-based detection method is that it leads to a low number of false alarms. However, signature-based IDSs are not able to detect new or variant forms of known attacks.

Most recently, network-based IDSs start to deal with big data, which also exhibit unique characteristics as compared to traditional data. Big data are commonly known as unstructured with various types, and it retain a need of real-time analysis (Hu et al., 2014). This development calls for new IDS protocols and architectures for data acquisition, real-timing data learning, and large-scale data processing mechanisms. One simple and classical approach to speed up data learning process is to apply PCA algorithm (James et al., 2013), which conducts a dimension reduction process on major high-dimensional datasets. When it comes to big data applications, PCA is also a great approach to perform for the sake of less memory consumption, less disk space occupancy, and faster processing on statistical learning algorithms. However, as pointed out by Pascoal et al. (2012), classical PCA algorithm suffers from a list of limitations, one of which states that PCA may act sensitively to the presence of outliers remained in the dataset.

6.1.1 Related Work

As pointed out by Xu et al. (2014), the security concerns of big data applications are from various roles, such as the data provider, collector, miner, and decision-maker. In a recent work (Rettig et al., 2015), the authors presented online anomaly detection over big data streams, which is a key part for between data provider and collector. Kim et al. (2015) introduced an anomaly detection approach to learn behaviors from big data storage such as various logs, which is also a critical chain for data collectors.

Some of the related research findings have presented on detecting anomalous behaviors and building robust PCs. Becker and Gather (1999) introduced the masking effect that illustrates the reason that traditional computations on mean and covariance matrix are not usually able to detect multivariate-based outliers. In Pascoal et al. (2012), the authors presented robust feature selection and robust PCA for the detection of Internet traffic anomaly. Pascoal et al. (2010) presented a simulation study of detecting outliers by robust PCA.

In summary, several research articles have presented robust PCA-based anomaly detection schemes for big data applications; however, the algorithm complexity is quite high, few of them have developed a lightweight scheme to deal with big data applications. The authors from Filzmoser et al. (2008) and Pascoal et al. (2012) have adopted robust statistical concepts such as median and MAD (median absolute deviation) to perform outlier detection; however, MAD is usually applied on symmetric distributions. Additionally, few of them have incorporated real-time learning schemes.

To fill in such a gap, a new approach to detect anomalies based on a robust pre-processing scheme for big data applications is proposed. In this work, a data-driven pre-processing scheme is introduced. It incorporates a dimension reduction algorithm and a real-time learning method. Specifically, the extensive use of robust processing is made to build robust principal components (PCs) and utilize real-time data learning to speed up the process. The real-time learning method is inspired by online learning, which differs from batch data learning that performs data learning in an entire batch of dataset. Real-time learning aims to make progress with each example it looks at. The working flow of our mechanism is presented in Figure 6.1.

6.1.2 Principal Component Analysis

PCA is mainly adopted as a dimension reduction technique. In the case of a real-world application, peoples' ability to visualize data is usually limited to three or less than three dimensions. With the use of PCA, it could significantly reduce the computational time of some numerical algorithms while the generated lower dimension data could be used to visualize the process.

In a data X with n observations (rows) with a set of p variables (columns), PCA will project this p dimensional data into a k dimensional subspace $(k < p)$ in a way that it minimizes the sum of squared distances from the

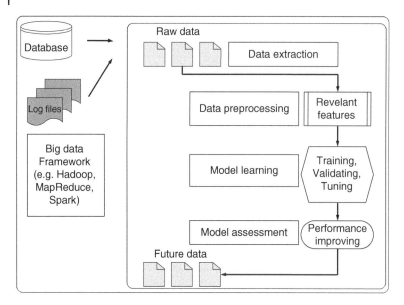

Figure 6.1 Workflow of big data framework and data learning process.

points to their projections. If the first k PCs are picked, the p dimensional data are projected into a k dimensional subspace.

During the projection, some of the information will be lost. Therefore, the concept of proportion of variance explained (PVE) (James et al., 2013) is used to present the fraction of variances explained by the mth PC to the total variance

$$\text{PVE}_m = \frac{\sum_{i=1}^{n} \left(\sum_{j=1}^{p} \phi_{jm} x_{ij} \right)^2}{\sum_{j=1}^{p} \sum_{i=1}^{n} x_{ij}^2}, \tag{6.1}$$

where ϕ_{jm} is the element of the PC loading vector ϕ_j. From the mathematical point of view, PCA seeks to maximize the variance of uncorrelated linear combinations from the original variables by forming PCs. In a simple illustration, a smaller number but highly informative k PCs explain the major proportion of the total variance of the p original variables.

6.2 Proposed Pre-processing Scheme for Anomaly Detection

The use of anomaly detection is motivated by the observation that malicious attacks are much more common nowadays and they exhibit distinctive orders. The objective is to explore the properties of PCs to identify outliers in the transformed space, which would not only produce robust PCs but also lead to significant computational advantages for large-scale data. From this perspective, a data-driven anomaly detection scheme is proposed on building robust PCs. An idea on real-time processing is discussed for the further use of this scheme.

6.2.1 Robust Pre-processing Scheme

In the first step of the proposed scheme, the log transformation is applied on the original numerical data X with n observations and p features. Applying log transformation can make highly skewed distributions less skewed. This is also significant for both making patterns in the data more interpretable and for helping to meet the assumptions of inferential statistics (Lane, 2003).

Once log transformation is performed, the second step is to identify the distribution of a given data. If the given data follows or appropriately follows the normal distribution, then robust statistical concepts, such as median and MAD, can be applied to process the data. If not, the idea of robust estimator S_n is adopted to process the transformed data. The identification of data following a normal distribution or not is beyond the scope of this study.

S_n, denoted as $S_n = c \cdot \text{med}_i\{\text{med}_j |x_i - x_j|\}$, was proposed by Rousseeuw and Croux (1993) as an alternative to the MAD. It performs well not only on the normal data but also on the non-normal data. S_n attains a Gaussian efficiency of 58%, whereas MAD attains 37%. The robust estimator S_n is used in this step.

In the third step, the log-transformed data are scaled using the idea of coordinate-wise median and robust estimator. The given data are robustly scaled in two ways. If the given log-transformed data possess a density of normal distribution, then the given data are scaled following $\frac{X - \text{med}_i(x)}{\text{MAD}(X)}$. If the given log-transformed data possess a density of non-normal distribution, then the given data are scaled following $\frac{X - \text{med}_i(x)}{S_n(X)}$. In this way, the mean operation is replaced by the process of median, and similarly the empirical standard deviation by the MAD and S_n. This provides newly and robustly generated data X'.

Then, PCA is applied to conduct dimension reduction on X' in the fourth step. The goal of PCA is to minimize the information loss, which is equivalent to the projection error. The square project error is minimized by $\|X' - X'vv^T\|^2$, where v is the unit vector of the first PC. This error can be represented by the trace of two products, denoted as $\text{tr}((X' - X'vv^T) (X' - X'vv^T)^T)$. By calculation, this yields $c \cdot (1 - v^T \Sigma v)$, where c is a constant value. This form is then equivalent to maximize the $v^T \Sigma v$, which is the covariance matrix. Singular value decomposition (SVD) is applied on the covariance matrix Σ to obtain the robust PCs.

The number of robust PCs that need to be determined is chosen in the fifth step. Ideally, the most percentage of the total variance should be retained by as many PCs as possible. However, this may not be the case as different applications possess different requirements. Assuming that at least an $\alpha\%$ of total variance is required to retain, then k is denoted as the number of PCs retained to satisfy this requirement. The project data after PCA is denoted as Z with n observations and k features.

Based on the previous step, the scheme is concluded by computing the squared MD of data Z. A quantile of χ_k^2 distribution (Pascoal et al., 2012) is adopted for the distance metric as a separation boundary for outliers.

The aforementioned scheme is the general idea to detect anomalies, even when new types of anomalies (attacks) appeared, this method can still be used to perform anomaly detection. Figures 6.2–6.5 show a visualized process on building robust PCs on a data with two features that normally distributed. The results utilize the 0.975 quantile to identify the outliers.

6.2.2 Real-Time Processing

Opposed to offline learning, it has growing strong interests in real-time (online)-based anomaly detection. The goal of online detection is to make a

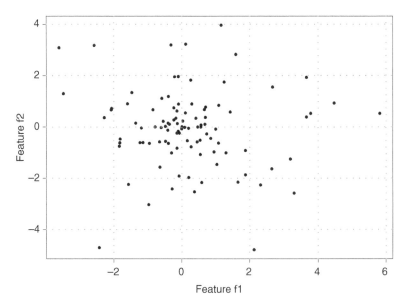

Figure 6.2 Standardized data.

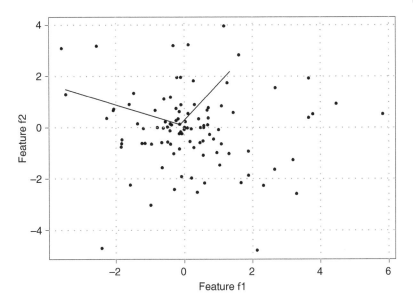

Figure 6.3 Standardized data with robust principal components.

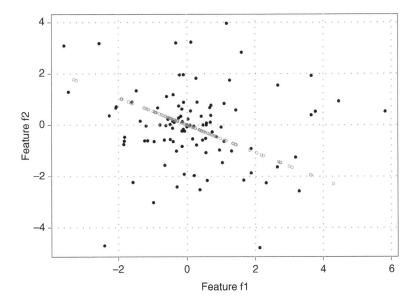

Figure 6.4 Projected data with robust principal component space.

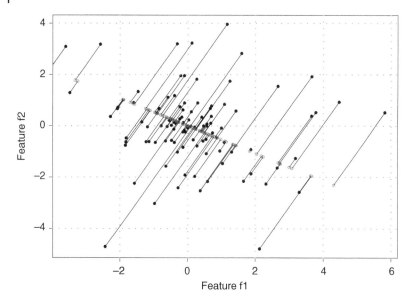

Figure 6.5 Projected data and standardized data.

sequence of accurate predictions given the knowledge of the correct answer to previous prediction tasks and additional information.

Online gradient descent algorithm is usually adopted by statistical models to initialize the parameter vectors and it descends along the gradient of the error function until reaching the minimum error. With a huge amount of data, it typically adopts an online algorithm that visits each data observation once or a few times rather than sampling a smaller batch that can be processed with batch algorithms.

Once given a new observation x_{new}, the learned statistical model f^* would learn from the new pattern and update the learning coefficients. In an anomaly detection example when $\mathcal{Y} \in \{0,1\}$, such process could be solved by logistic regression (LR) in

$$y_t = \text{logit}(\alpha_t \cdot \boldsymbol{X}_t + \epsilon_t),$$
$$\alpha_t = \alpha_{t-1} + \eta_t,$$

(6.2)

where t is the notation for iterations and ϵ is the residue between the actual and predicted value.

6.2.3 Discussion

The proposed scheme mainly adopts distance-based methods to perform outlier identification and to seek for robust PCs. The use of the MD shows robustness and removes several of the limitations of the Euclidean metric. It automatically accounts for the scaling of the coordinate axes, corrects for correlation between the different features, and provides curved as well as linear decision boundaries.

However, there were some potential drawbacks when the Mahalanobis distance (MD) was adopted. One of them is that MD may not perform well when the number of features is larger than the number of observations. This is because when a data has more numbers of dimensions than observations, then the covariance matrix will be singular, and a robust MD may not be computed properly. Additionally, high-dimensional data suffers from computational overhead rapidly with p than with n. The inverse of the covariance matrix performed in MD is a polynomial-based operation.

In summary, there is a price to pay for these advantages. The covariance matrices can be hard to determine accurately, and the memory and time requirements grow quadratically rather than linearly with the number of features. These problems may be insignificant when only a few features are needed, but they can become quite serious when the number of features becomes large.

6.3   Case Study

In this section, a case study is performed using the KDD data (Dheeru and Taniskidou, 2017). LR (James et al., 2013) is applied as a statistical method to find out the mean error rate. Both common statistical and computational metrics are used to evaluate the proposed scheme.

6.3.1   Description of the Raw Data

6.3.1.1   Dimension

This KDD dataset contains a total of five million records for the training set and 300 000 records for the test set (Dheeru and Taniskidou, 2017). These records were taken from the original 1998 DARPA dataset. In this study, 10% of the original data are chosen as our training set. In this training data, there is a total number of 494 021 observations and 42 features.

6.3.1.2   Predictors

Among 41 predictors, the first 9 predictors depict the basic features of individual TCP connections. The 10th to 22nd predictors describe the content features within a connection suggested by domain knowledge. The rest predictors show the traffic features.

6.3.1.3 Response Variables

The KDD data contain 24 different types of attacks. In summary, there are four main categories of attacks: (i) DoS attacks, such as the SYN flood attack, (ii) scanning or probing attacks (probing), such as surveillance and port scanning, (iii) remote-to-local (R2L) attacks, such as guessing password to unauthorized access from a remote machine, and (iv) user-to-root (U2R) attacks, such as buffer overflow attack to unauthorized access to local super user (root) privileges. As pre-processed work is only focused, these four types of attacks can be categorized into anomalous items, and then set the rest of the response variables as normal items.

6.3.2 Experiment

Feature selection on the data is first performed manually, and two zero-based features are removed. As the proposed scheme aims to conduct pre-processing on numerical data, the categorical features that contain in the original training set are then removed. There are four categorical features in the original training set, including the response variable. After performing log transformation, it is noted that the data do not exactly follow a normal distribution. Therefore, a robust estimator is applied to shape the data and obtain X'.

PCA algorithm is applied on the data before any model is run. Three robust PCs are chosen to explain the variance of X'. The first 12, 16, and 18 PCs are chosen to represent the cumulative proportion of approximately 80%, 90%, and 95% variance of X', as shown in Table 6.1. As discussed earlier, PVE is a term for visualizing the fraction of variances explained by the mth PC to the total variance. Figure 6.6 shows the PVE of each PC and Figure 6.7 shows the cumulative PVE of the PCs.

MD is then applied to the projected data Z. Figure 6.8 shows the density distribution of the squared MD of the entire Z. When the 0.975 quantile is adopted as the threshold to identify the outliers, 12 345 observations are found. Once the pre-processing steps are complete, LR is applied to detect

Table 6.1 Three principal components with their cumulative proportion of variances when α being 80%, 90%, and 95%.

	12th PC	16th PC	18th PC
Value of variance	0.925 87	0.774 61	0.706 64
Proportion of variance	0.025 72	0.021 52	0.019 63
Cumulative proportion	0.817 68	0.910 60	0.950 62

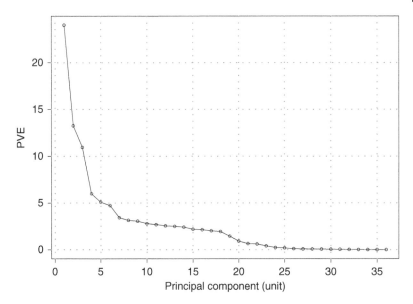

Figure 6.6 Proportion of variance explained.

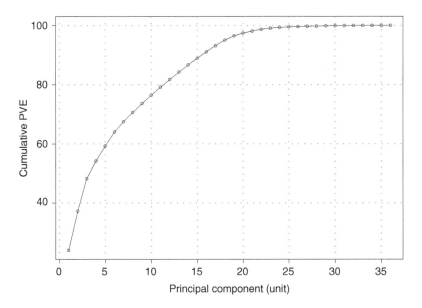

Figure 6.7 Cumulative proportion of variance explained.

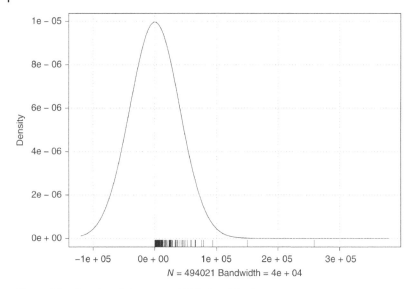

Figure 6.8 Density of the squared Mahalanobis distance.

the anomalies and compare the predicted result with the actual values from the response variable.

6.3.3 Results

In this study, a 5-fold cross-validation is performed to obtain the mean error rate. An experiment is run by LR using R (R Core Team, 2013), by a machine with a CPU capability of 6 Intel Xeon X5660 CPUs × 2.8 GHz and a RAM of 23.987 GB. The results are shown as follows: Once the proposed pre-processing scheme is performed on the data, the mean error rate is decreased by 0.6%, while the computational cost is saved for approximately 30 seconds, as shown in Table 6.2.

In Table 6.3, comparison between robustly dimension-reduced and original datasets is shown in terms of some common metrics. The first three reduced datasets retained a variance proportion approximately 80%, 90%,

Table 6.2 Results based on original data and pre-processed data (with all 36 principal components).

	Mean error	Computational cost (seconds)
LR (original data)	0.704 423 7%	228.060
LR (pre-processed data)	0.108 786 8%	197.556

Table 6.3 Metrics comparison: robustly processed data and the original data.

	12 PCs	16 PCs	18 PCs	Original data
Proportion of variance explained (%)	81.768	91.060	95.062	100
Computational cost (seconds)	164.236	212.896	227.824	228.060
Storage consumption (Mb)	47.8	62.5	69.8	374.4
Mean error rate by LR (%)	0.1042	0.0490	0.048 90	0.7044

and 95% of the total data. As the dimension is reduced, the computational cost is reduced correspondingly, as well as the storage consumption. In the example, the reduced data with 18 PCs only consumes 18% of the total storage occupancy, while it preserves 95% of the information. All the three reduced datasets retain a small amount of data storage consumption. The mean error rate of each data is also decreasing in general.

6.4 Summary

In this chapter, the study on an efficient pre-processing scheme for anomaly detection is presented. First, a few related studies and background of PCA are introduced. The proposed scheme is then presented. The goal of the efficient pre-processing scheme aims to achieve high detection accuracy and low computational overhead. Lastly, a case study is empirically conducted in terms of detection accuracy and dimensionality reduction.

References

Claudia Becker and Ursula Gather. The masking breakdown point of multivariate outlier identification rules. *Journal of the American Statistical Association*, 94(447):947–955, 1999.

Bruno L Dalmazo, Jo ao P Vilela, Paulo Simoes, and Marilia Curado. Expedite feature extraction for enhanced cloud anomaly detection. In *Network Operations and Management Symposium (NOMS), 2016 IEEE/IFIP*, pages 1215–1220. IEEE, 2016.

Dua Dheeru and Efi Karra Taniskidou. UCI machine learning repository, 2017. URL http://archive.ics.uci.edu/ml.

Peter Filzmoser, Ricardo Maronna, and Mark Werner. Outlier identification in high dimensions. *Computational Statistics and Data Analysis*, 52(3):1694–1711, 2008.

Han Hu, Yonggang Wen, Tat-Seng Chua, and Xuelong Li. Toward scalable systems for big data analytics: A technology tutorial. *IEEE Access*, 2:652–687, 2014.

Gareth James, Daniela Witten, Trevor Hastie, and Robert Tibshirani. *An Introduction to Statistical Learning*, volume 112. Springer, 2013.

Hyunjoo Kim, Jonghyun Kim, Ikkyun Kim, and Tai-myung Chung. Behavior-based anomaly detection on big data, 2015.

David Lane. Online statistics education: A multimedia course of study. In *EdMedia: World Conference on Educational Media and Technology*, pages 1317–1320. Association for the Advancement of Computing in Education (AACE), 2003.

Cludia Pascoal, M Rosrio Oliveira, Antnio Pacheco, and Rui Valadas. Detection of outliers using robust principal component analysis: A simulation study. In *Combining Soft Computing and Statistical Methods in Data Analysis*, (eds. Christian Borgelt, Gil González–Rodríguez, Wolfgang Trutschnig, María Asunción Lubiano, María Ángeles Gil, Przemysław Grzegorzewski, Olgierd Hryniewicz), pages 499–507. Springer, 2010.

Cláudia Pascoal, M Rosario De Oliveira, Rui Valadas, Peter Filzmoser, Paulo Salvador, and António Pacheco. Robust feature selection and robust PCA for internet traffic anomaly detection. In *INFOCOM, 2012 Proceedings IEEE*, pages 1755–1763. IEEE, 2012.

R Core Team. R: A Language and Environment for Statistical Computing. 2013.

Laura Rettig, Mourad Khayati, Philippe Cudré-Mauroux, and Michal Piorkowski. Online anomaly detection over big data streams. In *2015 IEEE International Conference on Big Data (Big Data)*, pages 1113–1122. IEEE, 2015.

Peter J Rousseeuw and Christophe Croux. Alternatives to the median absolute deviation. *Journal of the American Statistical Association*, 88(424):1273–1283, 1993.

William Stallings. *Cryptography and Network Security, 4/E*. Pearson Education India, 2006.

Shengjie Xu and Yi Qian. Quantitative study of reliable communication infrastructure in smart grid NAN. In *2015 11th International Conference on the Design of Reliable Communication Networks (DRCN)*, pages 93–94. IEEE, 2015.

Lei Xu, Chunxiao Jiang, Jian Wang, Jian Yuan, and Yong Ren. Information security in big data: Privacy and data mining. *IEEE Access*, 2:1149–1176, 2014.

Shengjie Xu, Yi Qian, and Rose Qingyang Hu. On reliability of smart grid neighborhood area networks. *IEEE Access*, 3:2352–2365, 2015.

Shengjie Xu, Yi Qian, and Rose Qingyang Hu. A data-driven preprocessing scheme on anomaly detection in big data applications. In *2017 IEEE Conference on Computer Communications Workshops (INFOCOM WKSHPS)*, pages 814–819. IEEE, 2017a.

Shengjie Xu, Yi Qian, and Rose Qingyang Hu. A study on communication network reliability for advanced metering infrastructure in smart grid. In *2017 IEEE 15th International Conference on Dependable, Autonomic and Secure Computing, 15th International Conference on Pervasive Intelligence and Computing, 3rd International Conference on Big Data Intelligence and Computing and Cyber Science and Technology Congress (DASC/PiCom/DataCom/CyberSciTech)*, pages 127–132. IEEE, 2017b.

Shengjie Xu, Yi Qian, and Rose Qingyang Hu. Reliable and resilient access network design for advanced metering infrastructures in smart grid. *IET Smart Grid*, 1(1):24–30, 2018.

7

Privacy Preservation in the Era of Big Data

The increasing attention on security and privacy has motivated the rapid design and implementation of multiple privacy-preserving methods. In this chapter, a few modern approaches for privacy preservation are presented. A privacy-preserving anomaly detection scheme is introduced to strengthen the understanding of detecting anomalous behaviors without compromising information confidentiality.

7.1 Privacy Preservation Approaches

This section presents five approaches for privacy preservation, including anonymization, differential privacy (DP), federated learning (FL), homomorphic encryption (HE), and secure multi-party computation (SMPC).

7.1.1 Anonymization

Anonymization is a technique used to hide an individual's identity while other information is exposed. For instance, the names of regular users could be hidden with an anonymized name or identity while their activities or transactions can be viewed.

Although the idea appears to be solid and privacy-preserving, the basic anonymization approach has been widely discredited because of the fact that the anonymized hidden data can be recovered (Narayanan and Shmatikov, 2006; Ohm, 2009). In one study (Sweeney, 2000), the authors discussed that 87% of the population in the United States can be uniquely identified using date of birth, zip code, and gender. As a result, more advanced anonymization methods were proposed, including k-anonymization (Bayardo and Agrawal, 2005), t-closeness (Li et al., 2007), l-diversity (Aggarwal and Yu, 2008), and DP (Dwork, 2008).

Cybersecurity in Intelligent Networking Systems, First Edition.
Shengjie Xu, Yi Qian, and Rose Qingyang Hu.
© 2023 John Wiley & Sons Ltd. Published 2023 by John Wiley & Sons Ltd.

7.1.2 Differential Privacy

DP is a technique to obscure individual details while preserving data patterns by adding noise to aggregated data. It is a statistical guarantee of the changes in probability of what can be learned by the addition or removal of any single individual's data (Dwork, 2008).

The amount of noise added is the value chosen for the privacy loss parameter. The more noise added to obscure details, the less precise data remains. The important balance to maintain is enough inaccuracies in the data to protect privacy while still providing useful information. For instance, the purchasing habits of a group of users can be analyzed to determine certain purchasing patterns. If 20 users actually purchased an item, applying DP to the data may show 19 or 21 users purchased the item. This makes it challenging for an analyst to know whether a particular customer purchased an item even if all other users' purchase records are known. The DP model protects against this type of deduction because the exact number of users and purchases are unknown.

However, there are some limitations in DP. In one scenario where precise data are needed, applying a DP technique is not advisable. This is well discussed in a study (Fredrikson et al., 2014), in which a Warfarin dosing model was developed using machine learning trained on data with various DP budgets. When the privacy budget was low enough to achieve meaningful privacy, the generated dosing model harmed theoretical patients.

In addition to the previous limitation, data leakage is also a concern. It can occur if there is too much correlated information for a single record. For example, if 1% of the users purchased a hiking gear and 1% purchased a map of national parks, an analyst could examine what other type of products were purchased by people buying hiking gear and national park maps, then check national park entrance pass holders for names of individuals who plan to hike in the national park. Although it causes a leakage problem, it can be mitigated by a DP guard, as shown in Figure 7.1. The DP guard acts as an intermediate node between a user and the server that stores data. A user who tries to analyze certain records sends query requests to the DP guard. The DP guard retrieves the data from the server and assesses the privacy impact of the queries. The DP guard tracks the cumulative privacy cost of all queries on that data to ensure that the privacy cost remains within the privacy budget so that the answers to different questions cannot be combined to infringe on an individual's privacy (Microsoft, 2012). The DP guard then applies the appropriate amount of noise to the query result and returns the noisy data to the user.

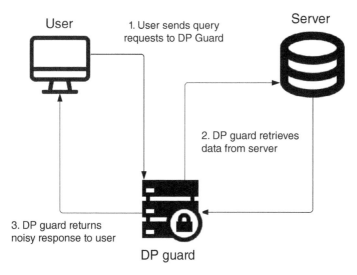

User

1. User sends query
requests to DP Guard

Server

2. DP guard retrieves
data from server

3. DP guard returns
noisy response to user

DP guard

Figure 7.1 Use of differential privacy (DP) in DP guard. Source: Adapted from Microsoft (2012).

7.1.3 Federated Learning

FL is a paradigm that trains machine learning models on multiple devices, preserving privacy by keeping the data on the devices and sharing only the model updates with a centralized server. This model leverages the computing power and storage of the end devices, eliminating the need to transmit a potentially large amount of data to a centralized server, and leading to the faster deployment of intelligent applications.

There are two major communication designs for FL, namely, centralized FL and decentralized FL (Li et al., 2021). In a centralized FL design, a centralized model is used to aggregate the updates from each training iteration. The initial global model is downloaded to each end device. Each end device then trains the model using local data and sends updated model parameters and training sizes to the centralized model. The centralized model then uses a weighted average to update the global model. In a decentralized FL design, the end devices communicate with one another, and each end device is able to update the global parameters directly.

In addition to that, FL can be classified as single party or multi-party depending on the number of entities that govern the process (Ludwig et al., 2020). As shown in Figure 7.2, one entity has authority over the data process and model design in a single party FL implementation. In the multi-party FL implementation, multiple entities partner with one another to train a shared model on their individual datasets.

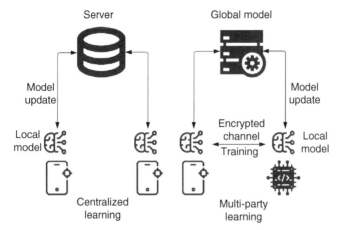

Figure 7.2 Federated learning models.

There are some arguments on the implementation of FL. One challenge is about the computing capabilities of devices that will conduct the local training. While some devices have sufficient computing capacity, there are some limitations on the device performance and battery level, further impacting the suitability of FL in most situations. Meanwhile, issues such as connectivity and bandwidth are concerns for FL, as it relies on frequent communications. These factors could potentially significantly impact the quality of the training, with scenarios such as failure to complete certain iterations during training. Therefore, one key research direction in FL is the study of robust and reliable training under heterogeneous networking environments (Ghosh et al., 2019; Nishio and Yonetani, 2019).

7.1.4 Homomorphic Encryption

Homomorphic cryptosystem is a semantically secure cryptographic system that allows certain algebraic operations carried out on the ciphertext to be performed directly on the plaintext. HE is a type of encryption that allows encrypted data to be analyzed without access to a secret key or knowing the contents of the encrypted data. Only the private key holder can view the unencrypted data and results. The typical use case for HE is when a data owner uses the cloud for processing but does not want the data in plaintext on the cloud. The data owner can use HE to encrypt the data, send the data to the server for computation, and then receive the results from the server with the data. The results stay encrypted, making it secure.

HE uses arithmetic circuits for additions and multiplications to determine the encrypted answer, with each round of interaction adding noise to the result. This means that with each computation, the results become less accurate (Acar et al., 2018). Mathematically, given a HE function E(), the encryption process is shown as

$$E_k(m_1 \bullet m_2) = E_{k_1}(m_1) \circ E_{k_2}(m_2), \tag{7.1}$$

without knowing the plaintext messages m_1, m_2 and the private keys k_1, k_2, where $\bullet$ and $\circ$ are different mathematical operators (Li et al., 2010). As the inputs are not being disclosed during algebraic operations, HE is practically used for privacy-preserving applications, such as secure e-voting systems, collision-resistant hash functions, private information retrieval schemes, and more. Microsoft Simple Encrypted Arithmetic Library (Microsoft SEAL) (SEAL, 2022) is an open-source HE library created with the intention of crowdsourcing a solution to make HE more efficient and easier to use.

7.1.5 Secure Multi-party Computation

SMPC is an encryption technique that allows mutually parties in an untrusted environment to compute a function on their combined secret encrypted inputs, creating a result in plaintext that all parties can view. SMPC not only aims to ensure input privacy but also output correctness by ensuring that colluding dishonest parties cannot cause honest parties to obtain an incorrect result. The classic SMPC example is Yao's Millionaires' Problem (Yao, 1982): two millionaires want to know who is richer, without revealing their actual wealth. SMPC uses arithmetic circuits and Boolean circuits and can receive input from multiple parties.

As shown in Figures 7.3 and 7.4, SMPC can be implemented based on secret sharing or garbled circuit (Evans et al., 2018). Secret sharing is when the input is distributed among all parties to compute locally before combining the local results from all parties to determine the final result. Garbled circuit uses a truth table to map the relationship between inputs and outputs, which is then garbled to use as a secret key.

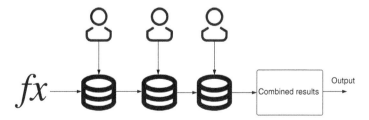

Figure 7.3   Secret sharing.

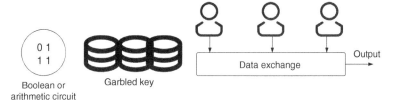

Figure 7.4 Garbled circuit.

Table 7.1 Trade-off: security and efficiency among privacy-preserving approaches.

Method	Security level	Efficiency
Anonymization	*	****
DP	**	***
FL	***	**
HE and SMPC	****	*

Table 7.2 Recommended use cases for privacy-preserving approaches.

Recommended use cases	Anonymization	DP	FL	HE and SMPC
Consumer preference survey	√	√		
Voting				√
Simple analysis of sensitive data	√	√	√	
Complex analysis of sensitive data			√	√
Sensitive data survey		√		√

7.1.6 Discussion

There is a trade-off for each approach between security level and efficiency, as shown in Table 7.1. The security and precision needs of a situation should impact the appropriate method rather than allowing the efficiency needs to determine the model. Table 7.2 presents some recommended use cases for various privacy-preserving approaches.

7.2 Privacy-Preserving Anomaly Detection

In this research (Xu et al., 2018a,b), a privacy-preserving anomaly detection scheme under E-Health system is presented. In the era of modern communication technologies and big data, E-Health has emerged and become a popular paradigm. Not only can the E-Health system monitor patients' health conditions continuously but also provides precise and efficient medical treatment accordingly (Abie and Balasingham, 2012). However, recent E-Health applications have raised serious concerns on detecting the anomalous behaviors in a person's sensitive medical records. Such records contain private data of health conditions, some of which are maliciously compromised and modified by adversaries (Barua et al., 2011). Existing research studies have investigated similar issues by incorporating multiple cryptographic schemes to guarantee the privacy of patients' sensitive medical records (Kargl et al., 2008). In this study (Xu et al., 2018a,b), a predicate encryption scheme for anomaly detection in E-Health applications is proposed. Specifically, the novel contribution of this study is the use of a session key as a message during the encryption operation in the predicate cryptosystem, in order to achieve both information privacy and efficient cryptographic computation. System model and security model are then described, followed by the design of predicates and operation stages of the proposed privacy-preserving anomaly detection scheme. Lastly, evaluation is conducted and the experimental results are presented in terms of overhead and accuracy.

7.2.1 Literature Review

As a popular cyberinfrastructure in today's healthcare world, the innovation of the E-Health system has facilitated many existing solutions such as health-care monitoring and health image processing and also expedited the process of medical treatments (Meingast et al., 2006). A wide variety of Internet of Things (IoT) devices are enabled and applied to offer continuous health services by collecting medical related data from wearable devices, analyzing and monitoring the data, and providing users' social interactions (Zhang et al., 2015). However, several privacy issues have appeared in many E-Health applications. One particular issue is the potential anomalous behavior launched against users' sensitive medical data, which is being maliciously compromised or contaminated by adversaries (Biswas and Misra, 2015).

In the recent research literature, a few articles have reasoned various anomalous behaviors and the popular algorithms to detect these anomalies. In Chandola et al. (2009), the authors presented a structured and comprehensive overview of the research on anomaly detection. In Xu et al. (2017), the authors studied an anomaly detection technique based on an unsupervised learning model. They examined the principal component analysis (PCA) model and proposed an efficient scheme based on identifying anomalies. In Kim et al. (2015), the authors proposed a method

Table 7.3 A sample of a packet from a user's health data and its critical component (heart beat vector *I*).

Time start	Time end	Period	Heart beats	...	Pulses
00 : 01	06 : 01	6 : 00	28 800	...	≈ 28 800
00 : 02	06 : 02	6 : 00	25 200	...	≈ 25 200
00 : 03	06 : 03	6 : 00	10 000	...	≈ 26 000
...	...	...	...	...	...
23 : 59	05 : 59	6 : 00	32 400	...	≈ 32 400

that recognizes cyber-targeted attacks and detects the abnormal behavior based on big data. In Rettig et al. (2015), the authors proposed a system that leverages both relative entropy and Pearson correlation coefficient for online anomaly detection over large data streams. However, those studies focus on anomaly detection over plaintext. Few studies target anomaly detection over encrypted data by which much sensitive information must be protected. Although some studies were proposed and discussed, a few of them that utilize encryption were mainly pattern recognition based with low accuracy.

Modern cryptosystem has brought a new perspective to address the challenge in anomaly detection over encrypted data. As a member of modern cryptosystem, predicate encryption is a novel cryptographic system offering precise, fine-grained control over ciphertext (Katz et al., 2008; Shen et al., 2009). By comparison, traditional public-key cryptographic system is dedicated to point-to-point communications, where ciphertext is prepared to the receiver who is already known to the sender in advance. In practice, the sender might want to define a certain policy that determines who is permitted to recover the ciphertext (Kim et al., 2016). In E-Health applications, a user's profile should be accessible only to the medical doctor who treats the patient based on their previous interactions, with no exception to other entities. Therefore, a certain cryptographic system such as predicate encryption is in need to address this challenge by offering more fine-grained controls over the ciphertext. As shown in Table 7.3, the packet data *P* is a sample from a user's health data, while the critical component *I* is noted as "Heart Beats." There might exist an anomalous behavior in this critical component on the third row. In that case, detecting such anomaly in a privacy-preserving way is the main objective of this research.

7.2.2 Preliminaries

The mathematical background of predicate encryption is presented. There are the bilinear group, basics of predicate encryption, system model, and security model.

7.2.2.1 Bilinear Groups

Let $\mathbb{G}$ and $\mathbb{G}_T$ be two cyclic groups of prime order $N = pqr$. A bilinear map e is a map $e : \mathbb{G} \times \mathbb{G} \to \mathbb{G}_T$, which satisfies the properties of bilinearity: For all $u_1 \in \mathbb{G}, u_2 \in \mathbb{G}$, and $s_1, s_2 \in \mathbb{Z}$, $e(u_1{}^{s_1}, u_2{}^{s_2}) = e(u_1, u_2)^{s_1 s_2}$.

7.2.2.2 Asymmetric Predicate Encryption

For a positive integer N, let $\mathbb{Z}_N$ denote the set of non-negative integers smaller than N, and $\mathbb{Z}_N^n$ represent the set of the n-dimension vectors where each component of each vector is in $\mathbb{Z}_N$. An asymmetric predicate encryption scheme for the class of predicates $\mathcal{F} = \{f_{\vec{v}} \in \mathbb{Z}_N^n\}$ over the set of attributes $\Sigma = \mathbb{Z}_N^n$ consists of four (randomized) probabilistic polynomial time algorithms: Setup, Enc, GenKey, and Dec, as described in Katz et al. (2008). The brief introductions are presented as follows:

- Setup: This step takes an input of the *security parameter* 1^n. It outputs the *public key PK* and a *master secret key SK*.
- Enc: This step takes as input the *public key PK*, the *message M*, and the *attribute vector* $I \in \Sigma$. It outputs the *ciphertext C*. This step can be written as $C \leftarrow \text{Enc}_{PK}(I, M)$.
- GenKey: This step takes as input the *master secret key SK*, and a *predicate* $f \in \mathcal{F}$. It outputs a key SK_f.
- Dec: This step takes as input the *secret key* SK_f and the *ciphertext C*. It outputs the *message M* or a distinguished symbol $\perp$.

For correctness, it is required that for all (PK, SK) generated by $\text{Setup}(1^n)$, all $f \in \mathcal{F}$, any key $SK_f \leftarrow \text{GenKey}_{SK}(f)$, and all attribute $I \in \Sigma$:

- If $f(I) = 1$, then $\text{Dec}_{SK_f}(\text{Enc}_{PK}(I, M)) = M$.
- If $f(I) = 0$, then $\text{Dec}_{SK_f}(\text{Enc}_{PK}(I, M)) = \perp$ with all but negligible probability.

7.2.3 System Model and Security Model

There are three distinct entities in the assumption of this research: a sender (provider), a receiver (examiner), and an attacker compromising the information at the sender's side. The system model and security model are presented as follows:

7.2.3.1 System Model

1. Trusted authority (TA): TA bootstraps the whole system and then generates secret keys to senders and the receiver.
2. Sender (information provider): In an E-Health system, the role of sender is represented by the patient. In this model, the sender has two tasks:
   - The sender creates a packet P, encrypts P with a session key K_s by Advanced Encryption Standard (AES), and delivers the encrypted packet P' to the receiver directly. The encryption process in this step is performed by the symmetric encryption algorithm AES.
   - The sender extracts a critical component I from the original packet P. The extracted critical component is treated as an attribute vector I. Both session key K_s and critical component I will be the inputs of a predication encryption at the sender's side. After inputs are encrypted by a public key, the ciphertext C will be forwarded to the receiver by the sender. The encryption process in this step is performed by the asymmetric predicate encryption scheme.
3. Receiver (information aggregator and examiner): In an E-Health system, the role of a receiver is represented by an information aggregator. In this model, a receiver has two tasks:
   - A receiver gathers ciphertext C from multiple senders and then decrypts C by key SK_f.
   - The receiver examines the critical component of a packet by validating the attribute vector with the predicate vector. If the process of validation is passed, then it means that the critical component of the packet is not contaminated. This also means that the packet is legitimate for the receiver to recover the session key and then decrypt the packet. Otherwise, the packet will be labeled as a potentially anomalous one.
4. Adversary (attacker): An attacker maliciously forges the sensitive attributes of the created packets and deliberately falsifies senders' packets with the contaminated elements of data (Figure 7.5).

7.2.3.2 Security Model

In this model, the receiver and senders are treated as honest parties. The attacker is treated as a malicious adversary and can only maliciously modify and forge the elements of an attribute vector I.

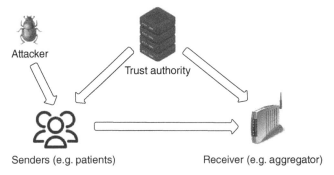

Figure 7.5 System model (Source: Microsoft).

7.3 Objectives and Workflow

The objectives of the proposed scheme are stated, followed by the workflow and steps.

7.3.1 Objectives

The main objectives of the proposed scheme on building predicate encryption for anomaly detection can be summarized as follows:

1. Confidentiality and privacy:
   - Confidentiality: The entire packet P is encrypted by a session key K_s. The newly encrypted packet P' is delivered from the sender to the receiver. Note that session the key K_s is not pre-shared between a sender and a receiver.
   - Privacy: As a part of the most sensitive information vectors, the critical component I of a packet P is extracted and treated as an attribute vector during the predicate encryption. The attribute vector I and the session key K_s are the only two inputs of Enc operation. Both of them are encrypted during predicate encryption and then forwarded to the receiver for further inspection and information recovery.
   - By the definition of predicate encryption, no person other than the dedicated receiver will be able to recover the message.
2. Efficiency: Contrary to a traditional way of choosing plaintext packet P as the input of "message" defined in the Enc operation, the session key K_s is adopted as the input of "message." In this way, encrypting a large file such as packet P' is avoided. In this way, K_s is protected by the predicate encryption system. Meanwhile, the legitimate, uncontaminated, and normal elements of data that satisfy the predicate function f can have the

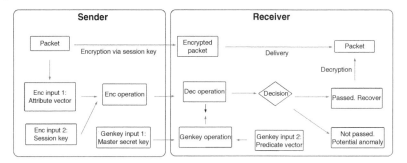

Figure 7.6 Workflow of the proposed scheme.

session key K_s recovered and decrypt the messages. This also shows that the session key K_s is not pre-shared between a sender and a receiver.

3. Anomaly detection: Whether a certain element of data being an anomalous one or does not depend on the designed predicate function f. The acceptance or rejection of the critical component I in this packet is decided by computing the designed predicate function. If it detects any contaminated and anomalous elements in the data, the packet will be labeled as a potential anomaly.

7.3.2 Workflow

The workflow of the proposed scheme is presented in Figure 7.6. Each step is illustrated as follows.

- Stage 1: Setup and Enc operations
  - Transmission input (session key K_s): The session key K_s is generated at the sender's side. K_s is an 128-bit or 192-bit AES-based key and is used to encrypt the critical component I of a packet P. In the context of asymmetric predicate encryption, the session key K_s is treated as "message" M.
  - Transmission input (attribute vector I): The critical component I is extracted from the transmitted packet P and then formed as an attributed vector I.
  - The initialization of security parameters shown in the step of Setup is also performed in this stage. Public key PK is generated in this stage.
  - Once transmission inputs are determined, the Enc operation is performed with the public key PK. This operation yields a ciphertext C.
- Stage 2: GenKey operation
  - Operation GenKey is performed by importing the master secret key SK and the designed predicate f (a designed predicate is used to check if there is any modification on the attributed vector, e.g. critical component). This operation yields a key SK_f.

- Stage 3: Dec operation
  - The decision is made by checking $f(I)$. If $f(I) = 1$, then the critical component I is neither maliciously modified nor contaminated. In an expression, $\text{Dec}_{SK_f}(\text{Enc}_{PK}(K_s, I)) = K_s$. Otherwise, if $f(I) = 0$, the decrypted information will be $\perp$.

7.4 Predicate Encryption-Based Anomaly Detection

7.4.1 Procedures

The detailed procedures of the proposed scheme are developed based on the predicate-only encryption system from Katz et al. (2008).

1. Setup(1^n): The setup algorithm performs $\mathcal{G}(1^n)$ to obtain $(p, q, r, \mathbb{G}, \mathbb{G}_T, \hat{e})$. Next, it computes g_p, g_q, and g_r as generators of $\mathbb{G}_p$, $\mathbb{G}_q$, and $\mathbb{G}_r$, respectively. $R_{1,i}, R_{2,i} \in \mathbb{G}_r$ and $h_{1,i}, h_{2,i} \in \mathbb{G}_p$ are chosen uniformly at random for $i = 1$ to ℓ and $R_0 \in \mathbb{G}_r$ uniformly at random. The public parameters comprise ($N = pqr, \mathbb{G}, \mathbb{G}_T, \hat{e}$) and

$$PK = \big(g_p, g_r, Q = g_q R_0,$$
$$\{H_{1,i} = h_{1,i} \cdot R_{1,i}, H_{2,i} = h_{2,i} \cdot R_{2,i}\}_{i=1}^{\ell}\big). \tag{7.2}$$

The master secret key SK is $(p, q, r, g_q, \{h_{1,i}, h_{2,i}\}_{i=1}^{\ell})$.

2. $\text{Enc}_{PK}(\vec{x}, m)$: Let m be the message to be encrypted, and $m \in \mathbb{G}_T$ (Zhenlin and Wei, 2015). Let $\vec{x} = (x_1, \dots, x_\ell)$ with $x_i \in \mathbb{Z}_N$. $a_1, b_1, b_2 \in \mathbb{Z}_N$ and $R_{3,i}, R_{4,i} \in \mathbb{G}_r$ are randomly chosen for $i = 1$ to ℓ.

$$C = \big(C_0 = m \cdot g_p^{a_1}, \{C_{1,i} = H_{1,i}^{a_1} \cdot Q^{b_1 \cdot x_i} \cdot R_{3,i},$$
$$C_{2,i} = H_{2,i}^{a_1} \cdot Q^{b_2 \cdot x_i} \cdot R_{4,i}\}_{i=1}^{\ell}\big) \tag{7.3}$$

3. $\text{GenKey}_{SK}(\vec{v})$: Let $\vec{v} = (v_1, \dots, v_\ell)$. This step chooses random $r_{1,i}, r_{2,i} \in \mathbb{Z}_p$ for $i = 1$ to ℓ, random $R_5 \in \mathbb{G}_r$, random $f_1, f_2 \in \mathbb{Z}_q$, and random $Q_6 \in \mathbb{G}_q$. The output is

$$SK_{\vec{v}} = \Bigg(K = R_5 \cdot Q_6 \cdot \prod_{i=1}^{\ell} h_{1,i}^{-r_{1,i}} \cdot h_{2,i}^{-r_{2,i}},$$
$$\{K_{1,i} = g_p^{r_{1,i}} \cdot g_q^{f_1 \cdot v_i}, K_{2,i} = g_p^{r_{2,i}} \cdot g_q^{f_2 \cdot v_i}\}_{i=1}^{\ell}\Bigg). \tag{7.4}$$

4. $\text{Dec}_{SK_{\vec{v}}}$: Let $C = (C_0, \{C_{1,i}, C_{2,i}\}_{i=1}^{\ell})$ and $SK_{\vec{v}} = (K, \{K_{1,i}, K_{2,i}\}_{i=1}^{\ell})$. The decryption step outputs m if and only if

$$\hat{e}(C_0, K) \cdot \prod_{i=1}^{\ell} \hat{e}(C_{1,i}, K_{1,i}) \cdot \hat{e}(C_{2,i}, K_{2,i}) = m, \tag{7.5}$$

and outputs 0 otherwise.

Scheme validation. Let C and $SK_{\vec{v}}$ be as defined before. Then,

$$\hat{e}(C_0, K) \cdot \prod_{i=1}^{\ell} \hat{e}(C_{1,i}, K_{1,i}) \cdot \hat{e}(C_{2,i}, K_{2,i}) \tag{7.6}$$

$$= \hat{e}\left(m \cdot g_p^{a_1}, R_5 \cdot Q_6 \cdot \prod_{i=1}^{\ell} h_{1,i}^{-r_{1,i}} \cdot h_{2,i}^{-r_{2,i}} \right)$$

$$\cdot \prod_{i=1}^{\ell} \hat{e}(H_{1,i}^{a_1} Q^{b_1 \cdot x_i} R_{3,i}, g_p^{r_{1,i}} g_q^{f_1 \cdot v_i}) \tag{7.7}$$

$$\cdot \hat{e}(H_{2,i}^{a_1} Q^{b_2 \cdot x_i} R_{4,i}, g_p^{r_{2,i}} g_q^{f_2 \cdot v_i})$$

$$= \hat{e}\left(m \cdot g_p^{a_1}, \prod_{i=1}^{\ell} h_{1,i}^{-r_{1,i}} \cdot h_{2,i}^{-r_{2,i}} \right)$$

$$\cdot \prod_{i=1}^{\ell} \hat{e}(h_{1,i}^{a_1} \cdot g_q^{b_1 \cdot x_i}, g_p^{r_{1,i}} g_q^{f_1 \cdot v_i}) \tag{7.8}$$

$$\cdot \hat{e}(h_{2,i}^{a_1} \cdot g_q^{b_2 \cdot x_i}, g_p^{r_{2,i}} g_q^{f_2 \cdot v_i})$$

$$= m \prod_{i=1}^{\ell} \hat{e}(g_q, g_q)^{(b_1 f_1 + b_2 f_2) x_i v_i}$$

$$= m \prod_{i=1}^{\ell} \hat{e}(g_q, g_q)^{(b_1 f_1 + b_2 f_2 \bmod q) \cdot \langle \vec{x}, \vec{v} \rangle}, \tag{7.9}$$

where b_1, b_2 are randomly chosen in $\mathbb{Z}_N$ and f_1, f_2 are randomly chosen in $\mathbb{Z}_q$. If $\langle \vec{x}, \vec{v} \rangle = 0 \bmod N$, then the above evaluates to m.

7.4.2 Development of Predicate

Two of the main constructions in a predicate encryption scheme are based on the set of attributes $\Sigma = \mathbb{Z}_N^{\ell}$ and the class of predicates $\mathcal{F} = \{f_{\vec{v}} | \vec{v} \in \mathbb{Z}_N^{\ell}\}$. As discussed earlier, $f_{\vec{v}}(\vec{x}) = 1$ if and only if $\langle \vec{v}, \vec{x} \rangle = 0$. For example, a four-dimensional long attribute vector $\vec{x}$ of a heart-beat dataset during a certain period could be in a vector like $[80, 90, 100, 20]$, where 80, 90, 100, and 20 are values collected in period 1 (T_1), period 2 (T_2), period 3 (T_3), and period 4 (T_4), respectively. The predicate function is defined as follows:

$$f([x | x \in [a', b']]) = \begin{cases} 1, & x = \text{Abnormality}, \\ 0, & x = \text{Normality}, \end{cases} \tag{7.10}$$

where a' and b' represent the minimum and maximum value of a legitimate range of a heart beat data in a period, respectively. In an example, let $a' = 80$ and $b' = 100$, the inner product of $\vec{x}$ and $\vec{v}$ would be $80 \cdot 0 = 0$ for period 1, $90 \cdot 0 = 0$ for period 2, $100 \cdot 0 = 0$ for period 3, and $20 \cdot 1 = 20$ for period 4.

The computation between attribution and predicate is conducted under bit-wise operation in binary. Note that this example is merely for the simplicity of illustration; however, the dedicated policy should be designed and customized for specific types of attribution vectors and their applications.

As presented in Katz et al. (2008) regarding the inner product of attribute vector $\vec{x}$ and predicate vector $\vec{v}$: If $< \vec{v}, \vec{x} >= 0 \bmod N$, then $f_{\vec{v}}(\vec{x}) = 1$ (i.e. $f(I) = 1$), and $\mathsf{Dec}_{SK_f}(\mathsf{Enc}_{PK}(K_s, I)) = K_s$ is derived in Stage 3 of Section 7.3.2. Otherwise, when $< \vec{v}, \vec{x} > \neq 0$, then $\perp$ from $\mathsf{Dec}_{SK_f}(\mathsf{Enc}_{PK}(K_s, I))$ is obtained in Stage 3.

7.4.3 Deployment of Anomaly Detection

Here, a dedicated predicate is designed to check if there is any modification on the attribute vector I. In the case of medical records, the regular heart beat data of a user collected from earlier periods is in a range of $[a, b]$, while the new heart beat data reported by a user is x. Based on historical data, machine learning and other statistical approaches can be utilized to determine the legitimate range $[a', b']$ of this heart beat data.

In this study, one goal is to detect if any extreme event or behavior would occur to the heart beat data, i.e. when $x < a'$ and $x > b'$. There are two cases to be discussed, and the example of $a' = 80$ and $b' = 100$ is used for the simplicity of illustration.

1. Case 1: The newly reported heart beat data are way below the minimum of the legitimate range a'. In this example, the newly reported heart beat data in a period is 20 because of a possible reason that a malicious person commits some certain malicious behaviors and wants to forge less amount of one's heart beat data. In this case, one's heart beat data suddenly gets dropped as it is different from the minimum heart beats 80 learned from historical data.
2. Case 2: The newly reported heart beat data is way above the maximum of the legitimate range b'. In this example, the newly reported heart beat data in a period is 500, because of a possible reason that a monitoring device is under some system malfunction. In this case, one's heart beat data encounters a spike, since it is different from the maximum heart beats 100 learned from history data.

The proposed anomaly detection scheme should be able to settle the legitimate range of $[a', b']$ once given an attribute vector and classify this profile into a suspect group, if the discussed two cases occurred. Although the suspect could be still from a legitimate user, the goal of this work is to label any suspicious behavior of a profile into a suspicious group instantly if any is appeared. There are a variety of options available in setting the exact threshold of anomalies. That type of work is beyond the scope of this chapter. In this study, abnormality of a given attribute data is defined as those observations that lie outside $1.5 \times$ IQR, where the interquartile range (IQR) is the difference between 75th and 25th quartiles.

7.5 Case Study and Evaluation

A case study is conducted in the environment of an E-Health application. The proposed scheme is applied to investigate the performance results in terms of computational overhead, communication overhead, and detection results.

7.5.1 Overhead

Let $|\mathbb{G}|$, $|\mathbb{G}_T|$ be the length of an element in $\mathbb{G}$, $\mathbb{G}_T$, respectively, and n be the dimension of a predicate vector. The benchmark computation overhead of specific base cryptographic operations in the predicate encryption is based on Table II of (Fan et al., 2017).

Figure 7.7 presents the computational cost of encryption at the sender side. When several senders are communicating with a receiver, the encryption of those senders is performed in parallel. Figure 7.8 presents the computational cost of decryption at the receiver side. As a receiver is dealing with different senders, the decryption at the receiver side is performed in series. From both Figures 7.7 and 7.8, it is learned that the growth of the length of attribute/predicate vectors n increases the number of clock cycles of a CPU when the encryption is performed. Specifically, the computational cost of a decryption grows larger when a receiver is dealing with more senders.

As for the ciphertext, Figure 7.9 presents the communication overhead of ciphertexts generated with different types of "message." As the novelty of the proposed scheme is to introduce the session key K_s (with 128, 192 bits) for the "message" as an input in the Enc stage, the storage of a ciphertext is much lower than the traditional method, which considers an encrypted packet P' as an input for this "message." Figure 7.9 shows the efficiency of the proposed scheme.

7.5.2 Detection

The concept of anomaly detection is deployed by using a dataset (Data Source: Health, 2017). After applying IQR by ruling out everything outside the range of the 75th and the 25th quartiles, the anomalies are detected as shown in Figure 7.10.

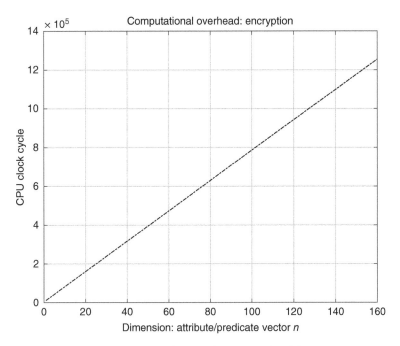

Figure 7.7 Computational cost of encryption at a sender side.

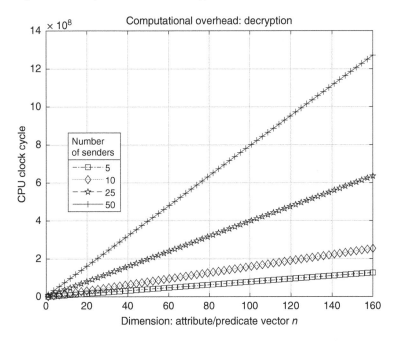

Figure 7.8 Computational cost of decryption at a receiver side dealing with different senders.

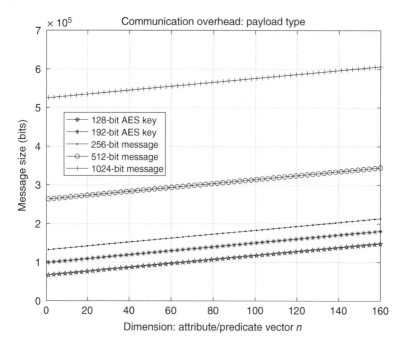

Figure 7.9 Communication overhead at the sender side for different types of messages: AES key and original message.

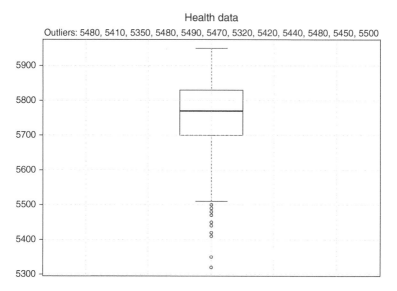

Figure 7.10 Detected anomalies by checking with the interquartile range.

7.6   Summary

In this chapter, a novel predicate encryption scheme for anomaly detection in E-Health systems is proposed. The novelty in this study is the use of a session key as a message payload during the encryption operation of the predicate encryption system in order to achieve both information privacy and efficient cryptographic computations. Moreover, the system model and security model are defined. Detailed descriptions on the design of predicates and anomaly detection procedures are presented. Lastly, evaluations are performed in terms of computational overhead, communication overhead, and anomaly detection.

References

Habtamu Abie and Ilangko Balasingham. Risk-based adaptive security for smart IoT in eHealth. In *Proceedings of the 7th International Conference on Body Area Networks*, pages 269–275. ICST (Institute for Computer Sciences, Social-Informatics and, 2012.

Abbas Acar, Hidayet Aksu, A Selcuk Uluagac, and Mauro Conti. A survey on homomorphic encryption schemes: Theory and implementation. *ACM Computing Surveys (CSUR)*, 51(4):1–35, 2018.

Charu C Aggarwal and Philip S Yu. A general survey of privacy-preserving data mining models and algorithms. In *Privacy-preserving Data Mining* (eds. Charu C. Aggarwal, Philip S. Yu), pages 11–52. Springer, 2008.

Mrinmoy Barua, Xiaohui Liang, Rongxing Lu, and Xuemin Shen. ESPAC: Enabling security and patient-centric access control for eHealth in cloud computing. *International Journal of Security and Networks*, 6(2–3):67–76, 2011.

Roberto J Bayardo and Rakesh Agrawal. Data privacy through optimal K-anonymization. In *21st International Conference on Data Engineering (ICDE'05)*, pages 217–228. IEEE, 2005.

Srijanee Biswas and Sohum Misra. Designing of a prototype of e-Health monitoring system. In *2015 IEEE International Conference on Research in Computational Intelligence and Communication Networks (ICRCICN)*, pages 267–272. IEEE, 2015.

Varun Chandola, Arindam Banerjee, and Vipin Kumar. Anomaly detection: A survey. *ACM Computing Surveys (CSUR)*, 41(3):15, 2009.

Data Source: Health. GitHub user selva86, 2017. URL http://raw.githubusercontent.com/selva86/datasets/master/ozone.csv.

Cynthia Dwork. Differential privacy: A survey of results. In *International Conference on Theory and Applications of Models of Computation*, pages 1–19. Springer, 2008.

David Evans, Vladimir Kolesnikov, Mike Rosulek, et al. A pragmatic introduction to secure multi-party computation. *Foundations and Trends® in Privacy and Security*, 2(2–3):70–246, 2018.

Chun-I Fan, Yi-Fan Tseng, Jheng-Jia Huang, Shih-Fen Chen, and Hiroaki Kikuchi. Multireceiver predicate encryption for online social networks. *IEEE Transactions on Signal and Information Processing over Networks*, 3(2):388–403, 2017.

Matthew Fredrikson, Eric Lantz, Somesh Jha, Simon Lin, David Page, and Thomas Ristenpart. Privacy in pharmacogenetics: An {End-to-End} case study of personalized warfarin dosing. In *23rd USENIX Security Symposium (USENIX Security 14)*, pages 17–32, 2014.

Avishek Ghosh, Justin Hong, Dong Yin, and Kannan Ramchandran. Robust federated learning in a heterogeneous environment. *arXiv preprint arXiv:1906.06629*, 2019.

Frank Kargl, Elaine Lawrence, Martin Fischer, and Yen Yang Lim. Security, privacy and legal issues in pervasive eHealth monitoring systems. In *2008 7th International Conference on Mobile Business*, pages 296–304. IEEE, 2008.

Jonathan Katz, Amit Sahai, and Brent Waters. Predicate encryption supporting disjunctions, polynomial equations, and inner products. In *Annual International Conference on the Theory and Applications of Cryptographic Techniques*, pages 146–162. Springer, 2008.

Hyunjoo Kim, Jonghyun Kim, Ikkyun Kim, and Tai-myung Chung. Behavior-based anomaly detection on big data, 2015.

Intae Kim, Seong Oun Hwang, Jong Hwan Park, and Chanil Park. An efficient predicate encryption with constant pairing computations and minimum costs. *IEEE Transactions on Computers*, 65(10):2947–2958, 2016.

Ninghui Li, Tiancheng Li, and Suresh Venkatasubramanian. t-closeness: Privacy beyond k-anonymity and l-diversity. In *2007 IEEE 23rd International Conference on Data Engineering*, pages 106–115. IEEE, 2007.

Fengjun Li, Bo Luo, and Peng Liu. Secure information aggregation for smart grids using homomorphic encryption. In *2010 First IEEE International Conference on Smart Grid Communications*, pages 327–332. IEEE, 2010.

Qinbin Li, Zeyi Wen, Zhaomin Wu, Sixu Hu, Naibo Wang, Yuan Li, Xu Liu, and Bingsheng He. A survey on federated learning systems: Vision , hype and reality for data privacy and protection. *IEEE Transactions on Knowledge and Data Engineering*, 2021.

Heiko Ludwig, Nathalie Baracaldo, Gegi Thomas, Yi Zhou, Ali Anwar, Shashank Rajamoni, Yuya Ong, Jayaram Radhakrishnan, Ashish Verma, Mathieu Sinn, et al. IBM federated learning: An enterprise framework white paper V0.1. *arXiv preprint arXiv:2007.10987*, 2020.

Marci Meingast, Tanya Roosta, and Shankar Sastry. Security and privacy issues with health care information technology. In *2006 International Conference of the IEEE Engineering in Medicine and Biology Society*, pages 5453–5458. IEEE, 2006.

Microsoft. Differential privacy for everyone. *Microsoft Corporation Whitepaper*, 2012.

Arvind Narayanan and Vitaly Shmatikov. How to break anonymity of the netflix prize dataset. *arXiv preprint cs/0610105*, 2006.

Takayuki Nishio and Ryo Yonetani. Client selection for federated learning with heterogeneous resources in mobile edge. In *ICC 2019–2019 IEEE International Conference on Communications (ICC)*, pages 1–7. IEEE, 2019.

Paul Ohm. Broken promises of privacy: Responding to the surprising failure of anonymization. *UCLA l. Rev.*, 57:1701, 2009.

Laura Rettig, Mourad Khayati, Philippe Cudré-Mauroux, and Michal Piorkowski. Online anomaly detection over big data streams. In *2015 IEEE International Conference on Big Data (Big Data)*, pages 1113–1122. IEEE, 2015.

SEAL. Microsoft SEAL (release 4.0). https://github.com/Microsoft/SEAL, March 2022. Microsoft Research, Redmond, WA.

Emily Shen, Elaine Shi, and Brent Waters. Predicate privacy in encryption systems. In *Theory of Cryptography Conference*, pages 457–473. Springer, 2009.

Latanya Sweeney. Simple demographics often identify people uniquely. *Health (San Francisco)*, 671(2000):1–34, 2000.

Shengjie Xu, Yi Qian, and Rose Qingyang Hu. A data-driven preprocessing scheme on anomaly detection in big data applications. In *2017 IEEE Conference on Computer Communications Workshops (INFOCOM WKSHPS)*, pages 814–819. IEEE, 2017.

Shengjie Xu, Yi Qian, and Rose Qingyang Hu. A predicate encryption based anomaly detection scheme for e-Health communications network. In *2018 IEEE Conference on Communications (ICC)*. IEEE, 2018a.

Shengjie Xu, Yi Qian, and Rose Qingyang Hu. Privacy-preserving data preprocessing for fog computing in 5G network security. In *2018 IEEE Global Communications Conference (GLOBECOM)*, pages 1–6. IEEE, 2018b.

Andrew C Yao. Protocols for secure computations. In *23rd Annual Symposium on Foundations of Computer Science (SFCS 1982)*, pages 160–164. IEEE, 1982.

Kuan Zhang, Kan Yang, Xiaohui Liang, Zhou Su, Xuemin Shen, and Henry H Luo. Security and privacy for mobile healthcare networks: From a quality of protection perspective. *IEEE Wireless Communications*, 22(4):104–112, 2015.

Tan Zhenlin and Zhang Wei. A predicate encryption scheme supporting multiparty cloud computation. In *2015 International Conference on Intelligent Networking and Collaborative Systems*, pages 252–256. IEEE, 2015.

8

Adversarial Examples: Challenges and Solutions

Adversarial examples are the latest cyber threats endangering networking systems. In this chapter, the concept of adversarial examples and challenges are introduced, followed by three research studies from both offensive and defensive perspectives.

8.1 Adversarial Examples

An adversarial example is an input to a machine learning model and its goal is to cause a misclassification after applying a small perturbation to the original input (Goodfellow et al., 2014). A use case in the computer vision domain would be taking a picture of a dog and then selectively modifying a series of pixels such that it still looks like a dog to a human observer. When supplied as input to the target machine learning model, the goal of the attacker may be to get the image to classify as a completely different object (e.g. human) instead of a dog (Figure 8.1).

8.1.1 Problem Formulation in Machine Learning

When training a machine learning model, the objective is to minimize the loss function so that the trained model will perform predictive analytics more accurately. Mathematically, the cost function C can be presented as

$$L_{train}(\theta) = \min C(\hat{y}, y^{true}), \tag{8.1}$$

where L_{train}, θ, $\hat{y}$, and y^{true} represent the loss value during training, model parameters, predicted value, and true label value, respectively.

Cybersecurity in Intelligent Networking Systems, First Edition.
Shengjie Xu, Yi Qian, and Rose Qingyang Hu.
© 2023 John Wiley & Sons Ltd. Published 2023 by John Wiley & Sons Ltd.

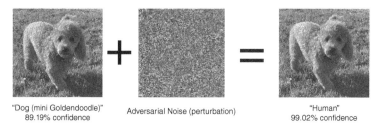

"Dog (mini Goldendoodle)"   Adversarial Noise (perturbation)   "Human"
89.19% confidence   99.02% confidence

Figure 8.1 Example of an adversarial example, inspired by Goodfellow et al. (2014).

However, adversarial attack is formulated in a similar way. Instead of minimizing the value of cost function C (also L_{train}), the attacker focuses on maximizing the value of cost function

$$L(x') = \min -C(y', y^{true}), \tag{8.2}$$

where x' is the perturbed data, which is the original data added with adversarial noise, and y' is the predicted value using perturbed data x'. Note that the negative sign in front of this minimization problem actually maximizes the value of cost function. Meanwhile, a constraint needs to be added in order to create a successful adversarial example:

$$\text{s.t. } d(x^{true}, x') \leq \epsilon, \tag{8.3}$$

where x^{true} is the original data and ϵ is the distance threshold set by the attacker to ensure that the original data x^{true} and perturbed data x' remain similar. Note that the distance d can be measured by l_2 norm, l_∞ norm, and others.

8.1.2 Creation of Adversarial Examples

There are multiple methods to create adversarial examples. In Section IV of (Yuan et al., 2019), the authors have described several approaches to generate adversarial examples. In particular, the authors in Goodfellow et al. (2014) proposed a fast method called fast gradient sign method (FGSM) to generate adversarial examples. Only one-step gradient update is performed along the direction of the sign of gradient.

8.1.3 Targeted and Non-targeted Attacks

Based on the adversary's specificity, adversarial attacks can be categorized as targeted and non-targeted attacks.

In targeted attacks, the adversary misguides the machine learning model to a specific class. Targeted attacks usually occur in the multi-class classification problem. For example, an adversary can fool an image classifier to predict all adversarial examples as one class. Targeted attacks usually maximize the probability of targeted adversarial class (Yuan et al., 2019). Mathematically, targeted attack can be formulated as

$$L(x') = \min \{-C(y', y^{true}) + C(y', y^{false})\}, \tag{8.4}$$

where y^{false} represents the specific class that the adversary dedicates.

In non-targeted attacks, no specific class is assigned by the adversary. The adversarial class of output can be random except for the original one. Mathematically, non-targeted attacks can be formulated as

$$L(x') = \min -C(y', y^{true}). \tag{8.5}$$

8.1.4 Black-box and White-box Attacks

Most adversarial attacks are black-box attacks, which assume the adversary has no access to the trained deep learning model. However, white-box attacks assume the adversary knows everything related to the trained deep learning model. In Liu et al. (2016), the authors presented successful approaches to transfer black-box attack method to attack a white-box learning model.

8.1.5 Defenses Against Adversarial Examples

In order to make machine learning generalized well during the testing and deployment phase, people usually adopt methods such as weight regularization, dropout, and model ensemble. Although adversarial examples occur during the testing and deployment phase, these methods do not work well to defend intelligent systems against adversarial attacks.

Generally speaking, two types of defenses are available, namely, passive defense and proactive defense. Passive defense aims to find the perturbed object without modifying the model, which is a special form of anomaly detection. Proactive defense aims to train a model that is robust to adversarial attack. In Yuan et al. (2019), the authors have discussed the details of several other approaches.

8.2 Adversarial Attacks in Security Applications

8.2.1 Malware

Machine learning models serve as powerful tools for detecting malware. However, they are extremely vulnerable to attacks using adversarial examples. Machine learning models that classify Windows Portable Executable (PE) files are challenging to attack using the existing methods such as Partial DOS Header manipulation (Demetrio et al., 2019) and FGSM padding attack (Kreuk et al., 2018; Suciu et al., 2019) because of the difficulty of manipulating executable file formats without compromising their functionality.

8.2.2 Cyber Intrusions

Adversarial attacks have also impacted the detection of cyber intrusions. In Yang et al. (2018), the authors studied the practicality of adversarial example in the domain of network intrusion detection systems (NIDS) and investigated how adversarial examples affected the performance of deep neural network (DNN) trained to detect abnormal behaviors in the black-box model. In Alhajjar et al. (2021), the authors focused on the attack perspective, which includes techniques to generate adversarial examples capable of evading a variety of machine learning models. In addition, the authors explored particle swarm optimization and genetic algorithms as tools for adversarial example generation.

8.3 Case Study: Improving Adversarial Attacks Against Malware Detectors

In this research (Burr and Xu, 2021), the difficulty of manipulating Windows PE files is examined for the purpose of creating adversarial examples. The research is proposed to develop more sophisticated attacks against malware detectors such as MalConv (Raff et al., 2018) and similar malware classifiers that take entire executable files as input. The objective is to discover attack methods that are much more sophisticated and difficult to detect than the current methods that simply append large amounts of specially crafted byte sequences to the end of the PE file.

8.3.1 Background

Malware remains a serious threat to both organizations and individuals, causing billions of dollars in damage annually as new trends such as Ransomware (Al-rimy et al., 2018) continue to emerge. Detection of malicious software previously relied on signature- and heuristic-based methods, and the volume of malware is growing far too rapidly to rely on these methods because of new variants appearing on a near-daily basis. The creation of unique signatures for each variant has quickly become an unsustainable task for effective malware defense.

Machine learning and deep learning models have emerged as powerful new methods for detecting previously unseen malware. Unfortunately, machine learning models themselves are vulnerable to attacks known as adversarial examples. While much of the research literature regarding adversarial examples focus on the computer vision domain, they can certainly be applied to security problems such as malware classification. The goal of this study is to develop new offensive capabilities against malware classifiers. There are many types of malware classifiers, often tailored toward a specific file type, such as PDF or Office documents. This study explores new attack techniques against executable files in Windows environments, more precisely known as Windows PE files. In particular, attacks will be tailored toward deep learning models whose input features consist of the full raw byte sequence of an executable file.

8.3.2 Adversarial Attacks on Malware Detectors

Attacks on image classifiers will output a perturbed image that can be used to attack machine learning models with the goal of causing a misclassification. This can be performed quite trivially within the computer vision domain, with the only constraint being that each pixel within a given image or video frame must remain within the valid range of values allowed by the associated file format (e.g. 0–255 for RGB images).

While any pixel value can be freely modified without causing the image to stop rendering, the same cannot be treated similarly about executable file formats. Even the slightest undesirable change to a field within an executable's headers or code section could render the malware useless, compromising its ability to run altogether (Kolosnjaji et al., 2018). As a result, many adversarial attacks on malware detectors and their machine learning classifiers are impractical in nature, often opting to output a representative feature vector instead of a perturbed executable (Park and Yener, 2020). Therefore, given the difficulty of inverse feature-mapping, it is not always possible to convert feature vectors into a problem-space object (Raff et al., 2018).

Although it is a more difficult problem to solve, practical adversarial attacks that result in perturbed executable binaries do exist. In a recent survey (Park and Yener, 2020), the authors identified 11 related attacks. They categorized the attacks into two distinct approaches, namely, gradient-driven approaches and problem-driven approaches. Gradient-driven approaches target white-box models by computing gradients, whereas problem-driven approaches target black-box models by editing

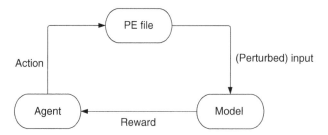

Figure 8.2 PE manipulation using reinforcement learning.

bytes and metadata, or by performing code transformations. In Figure 8.2, one example of a problem-driven approach is the use of reinforcement learning (RL) to reward agents for byte manipulations that cause the resulting executable to evade classification as malware.

Malware classifiers use both static and dynamic techniques for feature engineering. Examples of static features include hard-coded network addresses n-gram byte sequences, frequency analysis of system calls, and application programming interface (API) calls. Dynamic analysis captures similar features, but instead does so at runtime, first allowing the malware to unpack, decrypt, or deobfuscate itself. The environment can also be monitored to detect the behavior that static analysis may not accurately capture, such as additional processes that are spawned, registry values that are changed, or network communication that occurs (Park and Yener, 2020).

8.3.3 MalConv Architecture

This study focuses on producing adversarial examples against a promising malware detection model named MalConv, which uses the raw bytes of entire executable files as input. Prior studies require significant amounts of domain knowledge for feature engineering, whereas this technique seeks to minimize it. Most importantly, MalConv overcomes many of the challenges associated with previous n-gram approaches, such as their fragility with respect to single-byte changes and their overemphasis on manipulating PE header bytes (Raff et al., 2018).

Multiple studies have demonstrated that MalConv is vulnerable to adversarial examples containing byte padding at the end of the file, in part because the architecture does not encode positional information about its input features (Kolosnjaji et al., 2018; Suciu et al., 2019). As adjustments can be made to check for and counter such trivial modifications, research is needed to produce more robust attacks that utilize other sections of the

Windows PE file. Only three of the practical adversarial attacks surveyed by Park and Yener (2020) targeted the MalConv model, and all the three attacks used gradient-driven approaches to edit either padding bytes or header bytes.

8.3.4 Research Idea

This study aims to implement additional attacks against MalConv using both problem-driven and gradient-driven approaches. The use of semantically equivalent instructions within the code section is an area of strong focus, as more trivial modifications are well documented and limited in quantity. The ultimate objective of this study is to increase the sophistication of attacks that can be used against models ingesting an entire executable as a sequence of raw bytes.

The study begins with a thorough review of functionality preserving manipulations that can be applied to Windows PE files, including independent exploration to discover new methods and document semantically equivalent instructions. In addition to modifying the code section of the PE file, the following functionality preserving operations documented by Anderson et al. (2018) can be applied to increase the chances that the perturbed executable will evade detection: adding unused functions to the import table, adding unused empty sections, changing the name of the existing sections, adding bytes to the unused space at the end of a section, adding new entry points that simply jump to the original entry point, removing signer information, changing the debug information, packing or unpacking the file, modifying the header checksum, and adding bytes to the end of the file.

8.4 Case Study: A Metric for Machine Learning Vulnerability to Adversarial Examples

In this research (Bradley and Xu, 2021), a metric is proposed for quantizing the vulnerability or susceptibility of a given machine learning model to adversarial manipulation. The proposed metric uses only properties inherent to the model under examination. This metric can be shown to have several useful properties related to known features of machine learning classifiers and their enabled systems, and it is intended as a tool to broadly compare the security of various competing machine learning models based on their maximum potential susceptibility to adversarial manipulation.

8.4.1 Background

Recent studies in the field of adversarial machine learning (AML) have primarily focused on techniques for poisoning and manipulating the machine learning (ML) systems for operations such as malware identification and image recognition. While the offensive perspective of such systems is increasingly well documented, the work approaching problems from the defensive standpoint is sparse. In Suciu et al. (2019), Li and Li (2020), Yuan et al. (2020), Pan et al. (2019), researchers have shown attack methodologies specific to various malware classifiers using adversarial examples to force the model to label a malicious submission as benign. With this increased role comes an increased interest in targeting these machine learning models for exploitation and a greater cost when these systems are successfully exploited. Thus, research efforts in AML are relevant to stakeholders both in areas already using machine learning and those areas where machine learning is likely to become a significant factor in the near future.

Despite offensive-focused research, there have not yet been too many attempts to explore the problem from a defensive perspective. The objective of this study is to define a scalar metric that can be used as an upper-bound quantification of the overall vulnerability of a given machine learning model to attack through adversarial examples, with the goal of allowing different models to be roughly compared to one another through this metric.

In recent studies in Pan et al. (2019) and Creswell et al. (2018), the authors focused on developing attack methodologies against machine learning classifiers using generative adversarial networks (GAN), which exploit the mathematical properties of the target machine learning models themselves. The success of these attack methodologies shows a direct correlation between the physical and mathematical structure of a machine learning model (e.g. neural network) and its attack surface, thus justifying a defensive focus on the same properties.

8.4.2 Research Idea

The main task aims to measure the model vulnerability to adversarial examples. For a given classification model that considers n features and sorts them into m classes, an upper bound can be determined on the number of possible states, which is $\sigma = n^m$ distinct states. It is not suggested that all such states are achievable or reachable, only that they can be considered to potentially exist; thus, this metric should be considered an upper bound on the vulnerability rather than an absolute measurement or estimate. Then, a model that considers no features $n = 0$ would necessarily be no different from determining classification based on pure chance alone, and both the σ and λ of such a system reduce to 0, reflecting the inability of an adversary to influence a purely random result. The case of $m = 0$ for a model that classifies examples into 0 categories is outside the scope of this study.

It is commonly recognized that a *perfect classifier* is immune to attack through adversarial examples, as it is simply impossible for such a model to make an incorrect classification. Here, a *perfect classifier* is considered as the ideal machine learning model from a defensive standpoint, as it is immune to the types of attack under consideration. Therefore, the extent to which a given machine learning model "deviates" from a *perfect classifier* is of interest, as it is intrinsically linked to the potential exploitability of the said model. A value δ is defined to refer to the "deviancy metric," as the value expresses the amount of variation from a *perfect classifier*. This value is defined to aid potential future extension to machine learning models beyond classifiers. For classifiers in particular, the deviancy metric can be considered the sum of the type-I and type-II errors, representing the total probability the model will "mis-classify" a given input.

Given the calculation of the maximum number of theoretical states for a machine learning model and the definition of the deviancy metric, a vulnerability metric (or score) is computed, and it is based on the relationship between these two values. This vulnerability metric λ is defined as the number of possible states of the model multiplied by the probability of the model to return an incorrect prediction ($\lambda = \delta \times \sigma$), essentially a measure of the opportunities available to an attacker and the likelihood of a successful attack.

This simple mathematical definition can be shown to have several useful properties. For a *perfect classifier*, the deviancy metric is 0, and thus, the vulnerability λ will also be 0 regardless of the number of potential states in the classifier, matching the definition of a *perfect classifier* as immune to adversarial examples. Additionally, in an example of two models competing against each other, one model, which is more accurate (lower deviancy metric) but contains a greater number of potential states, can result in a similar vulnerability metric as the other model with a fewer number of potential states but a greater deviancy. This case enables the potential comparison of ML models based on their vulnerability to adversarial examples with a simple and intuitive "score." Finally, a machine learning model with the maximum possible deviancy $\delta = 1$, essentially a *perfect mis-classifier*, would thus have its vulnerability score represented by the maximum possible value for a model with the same number of potential states, which matches the expectation that such a model's vulnerability would be limited only to the number of possible inputs and outputs an attacker could influence.

Comparing competing machine learning models based on the vulnerability to adversarial examples can be performed by comparing the values returned by the proposed metric. This ties the vulnerability to adversarial examples to specific, intrinsic, and underlying mathematical properties of the given model and results in a single numeric "score" representing the potential vulnerability of a given model. Calculating the vulnerability in this way has been shown to have several useful properties that intuitively match the definition and expectations for classifiers.

8.5 Case Study: Protecting Smart Speakers from Adversarial Voice Commands

8.5.1 Background

Smart speakers, which wait for voice commands and complete tasks for users, are becoming popular to many households. With the advance of artificial intelligence, automatic speech recognition (ASR) systems enabled by machine learning models (e.g. deep learning) are powering the rapid progress and significant success of smart speakers with voice assistants, such as Amazon Echo and Google Home. However, researchers have recently demonstrated that deep learning, acting as the computation core of smart speakers, poses numerous security problems. In recent studies (Yuan et al., 2019; Akhtar and Mian, 2018; Rouani et al., 2019), the authors have indicated that deep learning is vulnerable to a well-designed input sample formed by adding small perturbations to the original sample.

More recent studies have shown that this vulnerability extends to the audio domain, undermining the robustness of deep learning models for the task for ASR in smart speakers (Wu et al., 2019; Carlini and Wagner, 2018; Chen et al., 2020). An attacker can manipulate a normal voice command by injecting a well-designed perturbation (i.e. a well-designed background "noise"). This perturbed voice command (or an adversarial voice command) appears to be extremely similar to a normal voice command, but it is actually a malicious voice command in disguise to easily fool deep learning models, rendering the smart speakers infeasible to function properly. Therefore, additional research efforts are needed to innovate the defense mechanisms against adversarial commands.

8.5.2 Challenges

Adversarial commands must be comprehensively investigated when designing secure countermeasures incorporating deep learning models.

Three main limitations are hindering the research progress of developing effective and robust defense mechanisms.

1. Most adversarial attacks are black-box attacks, which assume the adversary has no access to the trained deep learning model. This observation is commonly true for attacking real-time machine learning services. However, white-box attacks, which assume the adversary knows everything related to the trained deep learning model, are becoming popular and they can be easily transferred to attack black-box services because of the transferability of adversarial examples proposed by Papernot et al. (2016a).
2. Previous studies (Miyato et al., 2015; Papernot et al., 2016b) have attempted to make deep learning models robust to universal adversarial attacks. They considered the problem of constructing proactive countermeasures, but some of the proposed solutions were deficient as most contributions were based on modifications to the deep learning architecture. Such attempts can only partially prevent adversarial samples and they are far from being effective.
3. Because of the low-computing capability of smart speakers, previous attempts do not generally perform well for tasks under real-time scenarios, where type-I and type-II errors are increased.

8.5.3 Directions and Tasks

This research can be conducted from three different perspectives.

1. How to propose effective and robust countermeasures against universal adversarial commands to the audio domain? The most existing countermeasures to adversarial examples are studied in the image domain. Not too many studies have successfully addressed the issue with universal adversarial commands. If the defender's objective is to build a robust deep learning model, then it should improve resistance to adversarial examples regardless of application domains (e.g. image, audio, video) and adversary's previous knowledge (e.g. black-box or white-box attacks).
2. How to innovate countermeasures for resource-constrained IoT networking scenarios with real-time requirements? IoT devices for monitoring and tracking applications are usually implemented in low-cost resource-constrained embedded systems, which suffer from limited computing capability and only allow compact memory space (Aftab et al., 2020). Timely processing has been increasingly required on smart IoT devices, which leads to implementing near real-time information processing tasks as close to the end users as possible. It is challenging to implement

timely countermeasures in resource-constrained smart speakers against adversarial commands.

3. How to design and deploy a physical defense filter (e.g. "mask") which can be placed over the smart speakers, so that the over-the-air adversarial commands coming to the ASR systems will be filtered out? As the black-box services are enabled in smart speakers, it is infeasible for users to manually customize the deep learning models inside the smart speakers. However, users do have the option to deploy certain physical "mask" over the smart speakers so that a part of defense mechanisms against adversarial commands can be offloaded from the smart speaker itself to that physical "mask." A previous attempt (Yuan et al., 2019) was performed to place a physical filter in front of a camera on the self-driving vehicle to mitigate threats from adversarial image samples. Research efforts can be taken to investigate physical channels to filter out specific over-the-air adversarial voice commands.

This study includes four tasks: producing large-scale datasets for adversarial commands on smart speakers and examining the categories of the adversarial commands, developing a theoretical defense model against adversarial commands by innovating modern deep learning models, promoting the efficiency of countermeasures by analyzing the categories of adversarial commands with a list of priorities, and conducting simulations and developing experimental testbeds to validate the research hypothesis and evaluate the performance results.

8.6   Summary

In this chapter, the concept of adversarial example and challenges are introduced. With the discussed research challenges in both offensive and defensive sides of adversarial examples, three case studies are presented to highlight the importance of adversarial example research in the cybersecurity domain.

References

Muhammad Aftab, Sid Chi-Kin Chau, and Prashant Shenoy. Efficient online classification and tracking on resource-constrained IoT devices. *ACM Transactions on Internet of Things*, 1(3):1–29, 2020.

Naveed Akhtar and Ajmal Mian. Threat of adversarial attacks on deep learning in computer vision: A survey. *IEEE Access*, 6:14410–14430, 2018.

Elie Alhajjar, Paul Maxwell, and Nathaniel Bastian. Adversarial machine learning in network intrusion detection systems. *Expert Systems with Applications*, 186:115782, 2021.

Bander Ali Saleh Al-rimy, Mohd Aizaini Maarof, and Syed Zainudeen Mohd Shaid. Ransomware threat success factors, taxonomy, and countermeasures: A survey and research directions. *Computers & Security*, 74:144–166, 2018.

Hyrum S. Anderson, Anant Kharkar, Bobby Filar, David Evans, and Phil Roth. Learning to evade static PE machine learning malware models via reinforcement learning. *arXiv preprint arXiv:1801.08917*, 2018.

Matthew Bradley and Shengjie Xu. A metric for machine learning vulnerability to adversarial examples. In *IEEE INFOCOM 2021-IEEE Conference on Computer Communications Workshops (INFOCOM WKSHPS)*, pages 1–2. IEEE, 2021.

Justin Burr and Shengjie Xu. Improving adversarial attacks against executable raw byte classifiers. In *IEEE INFOCOM 2021-IEEE Conference on Computer Communications Workshops (INFOCOM WKSHPS)*, pages 1–2. IEEE, 2021.

Nicholas Carlini and David Wagner. Audio adversarial examples: Targeted attacks on speech-to-text. In *2018 IEEE Security and Privacy Workshops (SPW)*, pages 1–7. IEEE, 2018.

Yuxuan Chen, Xuejing Yuan, Jiangshan Zhang, Yue Zhao, Shengzhi Zhang, Kai Chen, and XiaoFeng Wang. {Devil's} whisper: A general approach for physical adversarial attacks against commercial black-box speech recognition devices. In *29th USENIX Security Symposium (USENIX Security 20)*, pages 2667–2684, 2020.

Antonia Creswell, Tom White, Vincent Dumoulin, Kai Arulkumaran, Biswa Sengupta, and Anil A Bharath. Generative adversarial networks: An overview. *IEEE Signal Processing Magazine*, 35(1):53–65, 2018.

Luca Demetrio, Battista Biggio, Giovanni Lagorio, Fabio Roli, and Alessandro Armando. Explaining vulnerabilities of deep learning to adversarial malware binaries. *arXiv preprint arXiv:1901.03583*, 2019.

Ian J Goodfellow, Jonathon Shlens, and Christian Szegedy. Explaining and harnessing adversarial examples. *arXiv preprint arXiv:1412.6572*, 2014.

Bojan Kolosnjaji, Ambra Demontis, Battista Biggio, Davide Maiorca, Giorgio Giacinto, Claudia Eckert, and Fabio Roli. Adversarial malware binaries: Evading deep learning for malware detection in executables. In *2018 26th European Signal Processing Conference (EUSIPCO)*, pages 533–537. IEEE, 2018.

Felix Kreuk, Assi Barak, Shir Aviv-Reuven, Moran Baruch, Benny Pinkas, and Joseph Keshet. Deceiving end-to-end deep learning malware detectors using adversarial examples. *arXiv preprint arXiv:1802.04528*, 2018.

Deqiang Li and Qianmu Li. Adversarial deep ensemble: Evasion attacks and defenses for malware detection. *IEEE Transactions on Information Forensics and Security*, 15:3886–3900, 2020.

Yanpei Liu, Xinyun Chen, Chang Liu, and Dawn Song. Delving into transferable adversarial examples and black-box attacks. *arXiv preprint arXiv:1611.02770*, 2016.

Takeru Miyato, Shin-ichi Maeda, Masanori Koyama, Ken Nakae, and Shin Ishii. Distributional smoothing with virtual adversarial training. *arXiv preprint arXiv:1507.00677*, 2015.

Zhaoqing Pan, Weijie Yu, Xiaokai Yi, Asifullah Khan, Feng Yuan, and Yuhui Zheng. Recent progress on generative adversarial networks (GANs): A survey. *IEEE Access*, 7:36322–36333, 2019.

Nicolas Papernot, Patrick McDaniel, and Ian Goodfellow. Transferability in machine learning: From phenomena to black-box attacks using adversarial samples. *arXiv preprint arXiv:1605.07277*, 2016a.

Nicolas Papernot, Patrick McDaniel, Xi Wu, Somesh Jha, and Ananthram Swami. Distillation as a defense to adversarial perturbations against deep neural networks. In *2016 IEEE Symposium on Security and Privacy (SP)*, pages 582–597. IEEE, 2016b.

Daniel Park and Bülent Yener. A survey on practical adversarial examples for malware classifiers. In *Reversing and Offensive-oriented Trends Symposium*, pages 23–35, 2020.

Edward Raff, Jon Barker, Jared Sylvester, Robert Brandon, Bryan Catanzaro, and Charles K Nicholas. Malware detection by eating a whole EXE. In *Workshops at the Thirty-Second AAAI Conference on Artificial Intelligence*, 2018.

Bita Darvish Rouani, Mohammad Samragh, Tara Javidi, and Farinaz Koushanfar. Safe machine learning and defeating adversarial attacks. *IEEE Security and Privacy*, 17(2):31–38, 2019.

Octavian Suciu, Scott E Coull, and Jeffrey Johns. Exploring adversarial examples in malware detection. In *2019 IEEE Security and Privacy Workshops (SPW)*, pages 8–14. IEEE, 2019.

Yi Wu, Jian Liu, Yingying Chen, and Jerry Cheng. Semi-black-box attacks against speech recognition systems using adversarial samples. In *2019 IEEE International Symposium on Dynamic Spectrum Access Networks (DySPAN)*, pages 1–5. IEEE, 2019.

Kaichen Yang, Jianqing Liu, Chi Zhang, and Yuguang Fang. Adversarial examples against the deep learning based network intrusion detection systems. In *MILCOM 2018-2018 IEEE Military Communications Conference (MILCOM)*, pages 559–564. IEEE, 2018.

Xiaoyong Yuan, Pan He, Qile Zhu, and Xiaolin Li. Adversarial examples: Attacks and defenses for deep learning. *IEEE Transactions on Neural Networks and Learning Systems*, 30(9):2805–2824, 2019.

Junkun Yuan, Shaofang Zhou, Lanfen Lin, Feng Wang, and Jia Cui. Black-box adversarial attacks against deep learning based malware binaries detection with GAN. In *ECAI 2020*, pages 2536–2542. IOS Press, 2020.

Index

a

Adversarial examples (AE) 1,
    113–124
  targeted and non-targeted attacks
    114
  black-box and white-box attacks
    115
Adversarial machine learning (AML)
    9, 10, 120
Anomaly detection 5, 75, 96–108
Anonymization 7, 91
Artificial intelligence (AI) 1, 2, 46
  trustworthy AI 6–7

c

Cloud computing 31, 32
Content delivery network (CDN) 33
Cybersecurity 1, 4
Cyber threats 17

d

Data-driven approach 4, 5, 37
Distributed Denial of Services (DDoS)
    19
Deep learning (DL) 2, 8, 9
Differential privacy (DP) 7, 92–93

e

Edge computing 31–40
Edge intelligence 36–40, 45

f

Federated learning (FL) 7, 23, 40,
    93–94

h

Homomorphic encryption (HE) 7,
    94–95

i

Information and communication
    technology (ICT) 36
Internet of Things (IoT) 31
Intrusion 17–19
Intrusion detection 1, 6, 22, 23, 56,
    76

m

Machine learning (ML) 1–5, 8, 9, 38,
    39, 113, 119
  reinforcement learning 4, 24–27,
    118
  semi-supervised learning 4, 22, 58

Cybersecurity in Intelligent Networking Systems, First Edition.
Shengjie Xu, Yi Qian, and Rose Qingyang Hu.
© 2023 John Wiley & Sons Ltd. Published 2023 by John Wiley & Sons Ltd.

Machine learning (ML) (*contd.*)
  supervised learning   3, 58
  unsupervised learning   3
MalConv   118–119
Malware   6, 19, 115–116
Malware detector   116–119

o
One-class classification   22, 59

p
Phishing   6
Poisoning attacks   20, 40
Predicate encryption   99
Principal component analysis (PCA)   47, 50, 75, 77
Privacy preservation   7, 23, 91
Penetration test   24–27
Perturbation   113
Pre-processing   38, 57, 78–80

q
Quality of experience (QoE)   33

r
Robust statistics   55

s
Secure multi-party computation (SMPC)   7, 95–96
Shellcode   19

t
Threat actor   1
Threat intelligence   49
Transfer learning   23

v
Vulnerability   119